Monetary Policy within the IS-LM Framework

Monetary Policy within the IS-LM Framework

Shahdad Naghshpour

business**expert**
Press

Monetary Policy within the IS-LM Framework

First published in 2014 by
Business Expert Press, LLC
222 East 46th Street, New York, NY 10017
www.businessexpertpress.com

ISBN-13: 978-1-60649-724-1 (paperback)
ISBN-13: 978-1-60649-725-8 (e-book)

Business Expert Press Economics Collection

Collection ISSN: 2163-761X (print)
Collection ISSN: 2163-7628 (electronic)

Cover and interior design by Exeter Premedia Services Private Ltd., Chennai, India

First edition: 2014

10 9 8 7 6 5 4 3 2 1

Printed in the United States of America.

To Ivylee

SN

Abstract

The majority of economists, would admit that money is powerful and that changes in money will impact the economy, to some extent and most of the time. Monetary theory analyzes and determines how changes in the supply of money affect the economy. The collection of policies that use monetary tools is known as monetary policy.

The main monetary authority of a country is its central bank. In the United States it is called the Federal Reserve Bank System (Fed), which is a federation of 12 Federal Reserve Banks. The Fed is responsible for initiating printing of money, monitoring the interest rate, and controlling the supply of money in the economy. Monetary authorities are shielded from executive branch interference by serving 14-year terms. This allows them to act without worrying about political fallout or fear of losing their jobs. The ability to work and function independently from political pressure has been used to claim that the supply of money is exogenous. However, the Fed acts in response to changes in the economy. It constantly monitors the economy and tries to determine the most appropriate interest rate and money supply; therefore, it is acting endogenously. The claim that the Fed's actions are endogenous does not mean that it is immune to errors, political orientations, or has full knowledge of exact amount of money necessary at every moment. Collecting and analyzing data takes time. Using monetary policy to achieve specific objectives, such as a reduction in unemployment and inflation, is even more complicated than determining the correct level of the money supply, or the most appropriate interest rate.

The collective response of economic agents to both economic and noneconomic factors is the expected outcome of economy, which is formulated as economic theory. Economic theory is not the product of economists' wishful thinking, or a purposeful design of a person or a group to create a product as in many areas. For example, computers are designed and created to accomplish a set of desired outcomes. Economics, on the other hand, involves understanding how economic agents react to factors that affect the economy. Economic theories, in turn, reflect how the economy functions and what causes it to change. Therefore, economic theories explain a reality that is the result of the interaction of people in response to changes in economic factors. It is not necessary to know economics in order to act according to economic theory any more than it is necessary for a planet to know the laws of physics to "choose" an appropriate orbit and speed for its position among other planets. In this context, the source of change in an economy is irrelevant; it can be endogenous or exogenous. However, whether or not government intervention in the economy is endogenous or exogenous is completely irrelevant.

Keywords

monetary theory, monetary policy, IS, LM, quantity theory, Keynes, fiscal policy, effectiveness of money, discretionary policies

Contents

List of Figures

Acknowledgments

I am indebted to my family for the time I took away from them. I would like to thank Candace Bright, Brian Carriere, Charles Tibedo, and Michael Webb, all doctoral students at the International Development and International Affairs at the University of Southern Mississippi. Without the help of these people I would not have been able to finish this book. Their contributions have been essential, and without their tireless efforts I would not have been able to finish this work. Any remaining shortcomings rest solely on my shoulders. I would also like to thank the following people for proof-reading parts of the manuscript: Richard Baker, Ed Bee, Dave Davis, Denise Francois, Madeline Gillette, Shawn Lowe, Pat O'Brien, Charles Tibedo, Michael Webb.

Background and Fundamental Theories

CHAPTER 1

A Brief History of Monetary Theory

Monetary theory seems to have existed from the dawn of modern economics. Although Smith's *Wealth of Nations*[1] is considered the foundation of the methodological study of economics, monetary theory was already well established by then. Here, the term "monetary theory" narrowly refers to the relationship between the supply of money and the price level. As such, Mun[2] states that exporting expensive, and importing cheap, would result in what is today called a positive balance of trade. He also points out that an inflow of bullion raises domestic prices; a fundamental conclusion of monetary theory. The direct relationship between the quantity of money in circulation and the price level, which was demonstrated by Locke,[3] is known as the quantity theory of money, which will be addressed shortly.

On the other hand, if by monetary theory we mean the theories that explain the role of money as an instrument to influence the course of the economy through a deliberate act of government, then the concept is more recent. Government intervention in the economy for the purpose of changing aggregate indicators falls into two distinct forms: monetary policy and fiscal policy.

Definition

Monetary policy refers to government intervention in the economy through manipulation of the supply of money for the purpose of influencing the course of the economy.

Definition

Fiscal policy refers to government intervention in the economy through manipulation of government revenues and disbursements for the purpose of influencing the course of the economy.

Whether the government should intervene in the economy is a normative subject. The present book does not address the wisdom of government intervention in the economy. Instead, it focuses on the effects of government on the economy, specifically the impact of money on macroeconomic indicators.

Definition

Macroeconomics is the study of aggregated indicators, such as gross domestic product (GDP).

Definition

GDP is the value of final goods and services produced in a country in one year.

Many early economics writings were about trade. Mun[4] points out that the value of exports must be equal to the value of imports for all countries. An increase in gold or silver, which was considered money at that time, will increase price levels in the country of origin, relative to the prices present in other countries. Consequently, exports from the country will decline and its import will rise. The resulting deficit requires an outflow of bullion. Countries that receive bullion face the same consequences. Their price levels increase, exports decrease, and imports increase. They, in turn, must pay for the deficit with their recently acquired bullion. The process continues until price levels have risen globally, and a new trade equilibrium is achieved corresponding to larger supply of money.

The relationship between the supply of money and price level is the cornerstone of the monetary theory. An increase in money supply will increase prices, other things equal. The term "other things equal" is crucial. When the supply of money increases the price level will increase, provided there are no idle resources in the economy. For example, an increase in supply of money when there is unemployment would increase output, not the price level.

Classical Economists and Business Cycles

A major problem for the classical economists is their inability to explain the existence of business cycles. Early economists and the classical economists after them were concerned with the long run since they wrote about economic growth. In the long run the economy is at the full employment level and also at equilibrium. These conditions do not allow for an economic downturn, which is part of any business cycle. Pre-industrial revolution economies were agrarian and were affected by natural disasters, such as droughts and blizzards, which have some cyclical pattern. In order not to stray into other fields of study and avoid being dragged into the discussion of whether or not natural disasters have specific cyclical patterns, we can assume they occur randomly. Natural disasters (e.g., droughts) affect the economy by hindering production, destroying property, wasting resources in recovery, and damaging capital goods used for production. In short, they reduce the production capacity of the economy. Consequently, they cause an economic contraction. Wars are also major destroyers of economic resources and cause downturns in economies. The Napoleonic Wars (1803–1815) caused a depression in the United Kingdom that lasted 13 years.[5] In general, business cycles were believed to be caused by exogenous factors. A notable, and oft-repeated, example is Jevons's[6] explanation of business cycles using the sunspots activities. The idea is defendable to some extent since sunspots are the result of changes in the temperature on the sun's surface, which directly impacts earth's climate. The claim was poorly stated and evidenced, causing it to fail to apply to any country other than the Great Britain. However, the effects of natural disasters on the economy have diminished considerably since industrialization, because modern manufacturing processes do not depend on climatic conditions. One exception is the destruction of production facility by a storm.

What is (Modern) Monetary Theory?

Monetary theory is the collection of theories about money that provide theoretical foundations for monetary policies. This theory provides an expected outcome for specific monetary policies. When economic indicators, such as unemployment or inflation, are not at a desired level, the government can change monetary instruments, such as the supply of money, to reduce unemployment or inflation. This is the view of advocates of monetary policy. The quantity theory of money, which will be discussed in the next section, is the most prominent component of the subject.

When early economists addressed the effect of money on the economy they focused on economic growth, which is a long run issue and pertains to equilibrium, rather than disequilibrium, which is a short run problem. This view is expressed in the introduction of the *Wealth of Nations*.[7] Many early economists did not even acknowledge the possibility of disequilibrium, in part due to misinterpretation of Say's Law. Economic downturns associated with business cycles were considered temporary and attributed to the external forces.[8] This should not be interpreted as a lack of awareness of business cycles by the classical economists. In fact, studies of business cycles stretch back to at least 18th[9] and 19th centuries.[10]

Definition

Say's Law of Market states that production creates its own demand.

In other words, production generates sufficient income to generate enough demand for itself. According to Say, "products are paid for by products." This statement is a macroeconomic statement at heart. Say's Law links production in one industry to demand generated by income created in other industries. Although it is possible to produce too little or too much in one industry or sector, it is not possible to do so at the level of national economy. A misinterpretation of Say's Law is the notion that whatever is produced will be sold. Any bankrupt businessman that could not sell his product would testify to the fallacy of the argument. Aggregate demand and aggregate supply are not independent from each other; they are determined endogenously. Thus, what is true at the microeconomic level need not be, and often is not, necessarily true at the macroeconomic level. It is important to realize the argument that both supply and demand are determined exogenously, is valid only in a barter economy.

Definition

Barter is the exchange of one thing for another, when neither good is "money."

Say's law ignores the role of money. In order to have over or under production a point of reference is needed, which is provided by money. Money does not exist in a barter economy; hence, in barter economies aggregate production must equal aggregate demand. However, this is not necessarily true in an economy that functions via money. In order to have an excess supply of something there must be an excess demand for something else. In a barter economy it is impossible to have an excess aggregate supply over aggregate demand for all goods. On the other hand, a general oversupply of commodities in a monetary economy implies there is an excess demand for money. This situation indicates a case of disequilibrium, which cannot persist in the long run. An implication of Say's Law is that the money market is always in equilibrium because money is only used for exchange, while goods are supplied to demand other goods. Patinkin[11] refers to this as the "dichotomized pricing process," whereby classical and neoclassical economists use relative prices in commodity markets (homogeneity postulate) and absolute prices (or nominal) in the money market in their analyses. These aggregate analyses became the foundations of macroeconomics and the center point of the IS–LM analysis, which is covered in Chapter 3.

Nevertheless, Say's Law is a valid comparative static tool. Keynes' opposition to the Say's Law stems from the fact that full equilibrium is a dynamic process; although it is pursued constantly it is never achieved. The process of pursing equilibrium may displace the equilibrium point.

Definition

Comparative statics analysis compares two static equilibria without attention to how the market moves from one equilibrium point to another.

Definition

Dynamic analysis explains the path from one equilibrium point to another providing a causal relationship.

The Quantity Theory of Money

Although the concept of the quantity theory of money dates back to Mun,[12] its formulation is credited to Irving Fisher of the 20th century.

Fisher's approach, which is often referred to as the **transaction approach** to the quantity theory of money, defines the demand for money from a macroeconomics perspective. The model ascertains that the demand for money is a multiple of total money expenditures (price times output), which in turn, is nominal GDP. The "**equation of exchange**"[13] is:

$$MV \equiv PQ$$

(1.1)

where V is the velocity of money (M), which is assumed to be fairly stable over time for a given economy, P is the price level or average price, and Q is the output of the economy, at least in a closed economy.[14] The symbol consisting of three bars (\[\equiv \]) represents an identity. The identity indicates that the left side is identical to the right side. However, identities are not equations, and there is no causal relationship between the two sides of an identity.

Definition

The **velocity** of money represents the average number of times money changes hand in a year.

The quantity theory of money is the doctrine that links money to prices, while prices are determined by real forces of the economy, assuming that economic institutions in the economy remain the same. Note that the equation of exchange must always be true regardless of the state of the economy. By virtue of the fact that the right-hand side represents the value of the transactions, the transactions must have taken place, and payment received. Thus, the amount of money that paid for the transaction, that is, the actual amount of money multiplied by the number of times it changed hands, must be of the same magnitude. This is what makes the equation of exchange an identity.

Mercantilists use money to explain trade rather than prices. In his statements such as "money stimulates trade," Locke means that the price level is always proportionate to the quantity of money. It was understood that the quantity of money included the quickness of its circulation, or its velocity. Although Locke's statement is true, it is not a theory.

In this presentation, money is nothing more than a **medium of exchange**; hence, it has no intrinsic value. Hume[15] argues that trade and velocity are not sensitive to changes in the money supply, which only changes prices. Notwithstanding causality, the statement is true if money is a **standard of value** and a **medium of exchange**. However, the argument fails as soon as money is demanded as a **store of value**, that is, money and price levels do not necessarily vary proportionately. For more detail about the roles of money see Naghshpour.[16] The problem in understanding why money and prices do not vary proportionately arises from confusion between comparative static analysis and dynamic analysis.

The effect of an increase in the supply of money is similar to an increase in its velocity; a fact that Cantillon demonstrates as early as 1720; although his work was not published until 1755. Cantillon also points out Locke's failure in explaining how an increase in money leads to an increase in prices. This failure is at the heart of the application of the quantity theory in monetary policy, where it is necessary to know by how much to increase the supply of money for a specific increase in prices. Cantillon states that an increase in supply of money will not merely raise price levels, but also alter the structure of prices. Keynes[17] refers to this **Cantillon effect** in his critique of the quantity theory.

It is important to understand that the quantity theory of money is a macroeconomic analysis. Another important issue is the role or power of money as a policy instrument. Hume[18] points out that the amount of money affects the economy; thus **"money matters."** Even if money matters, it is not clear what the extent of its effectiveness is. An essential variable in monetary policy is the **interest rate**. Classical proponents of the quantity theory argue that there is an inverse relationship between the amount of money in circulation and the interest rate. This is a true statement, but not necessarily for the reasons early economists provided. There are other factors that affect this relationship, including the preference for liquidity. More important to this discussion are the endogenous variables that govern investment demand.

Smith[19] distinguishes between different ways the money supply can increase in a country. When money increases due to discovery of new mines of precious metals or increased output of existing mines, the result is an increase in price levels. However, when a nation becomes more productive and as a result, wealthier, the money supply increases, but the price level does not. The distinction, which Smith does not point out, is that the former "money" refers to the supply of money while the latter refers to the demand for money. However, he is correct in his observation that in both cases the amount of money in circulation increases. Therefore, Smith[20] refutes the quantity theory in the case of fixed exchange rates; however, he cites the over issue of paper money as the cause of inflation in the case of British colonies in North America.

The discussion of disequilibrium, even in the 19th century, was focused on the excess of supply of money and was never about the shortage of money, which is possible in economies based on bullion. In such cases, the value of bullion would increase, which can be remedied by lowering the amount of actual gold or silver in the coins; something that has been practiced for centuries. The fact is that not only paper money existed in those days, but also fiat money, which prevailed at least from time to time.

Definition

Fiat money is a currency without precious metal backing. The value of fiat money stems from the dependability of the government that issues it.

One example of fiat money is the case of Great Britain between 1797 and 1821 when conversion of paper money to precious metals was suspended due to a shortage of silver and the high cost of the Napoleonic Wars.

Discussions about the consequences of an increase in the supply of money on the economy during the era of metal-based currencies treat it as exogenous. This would be a valid point under bullion-based currency and possibly limited to new discoveries of mines. Existing mines continue producing precious metals until their marginal costs equal their respective marginal revenues, which are determined in turn by the demand for money, as indicated by the right-hand side of the equation of exchange, which is the value of goods and services exchanged in the economy.

Definition

Marginal revenue is the increase in revenue as a result of producing one more unit of a good or service.

Definition

Marginal cost is the cost of producing one more unit of a good or service.

When marginal revenue is greater than marginal cost, an increase in output also increases revenue. Marginal revenue declines as output increases, which is a consequence of the negatively sloped demand function. Alternatively, marginal cost increases as output increases, which is a consequence of diminishing marginal productivity. Thus, an increase in output will eventually result in the equality of marginal revenue and marginal cost.

As long as the marginal cost is equal to the marginal revenue and the supply and demand for money are equal, there is no reason to change the supply of money from existing mines. When a new mine is discovered the supply of bullion increases, and its price decreases, like any other commodity. The presumption is that the marginal cost of the new mine is less than it is for existing mines. Otherwise, the new discovery will be deemed unprofitable and production will not take place. However, when the precious metal is used as money its value is reflected in the price of other goods that become relatively more expensive; a fact that early economists understood well. As noted earlier, Smith differentiates between an exogenous increase in the supply of money and an endogenous increase induced by greater demand for money as a result of an increase in output. The issue of exogeneity of money is an ongoing discussion, especially under the fiat money system; why governments would change the supply of money without an economic reason is a question that remains unanswered by proponents of the exogeneity of money. Even when the "reason" is misguided, the change in the money supply is still caused within the system, and is therefore an endogenous variable. The only time paper-currency money can be treated as exogenous is when the government sets the supply of money capriciously and without regard to economic considerations.

CHAPTER 2

Politics and Monetary Policy

Early economists were trying to understand the governing principles explaining how economies function. One of the most important and early issues was determining the role of money in the economy. The first view about money was that money is not one of the wheels that move the economy; rather, it is the oil that helps the wheels turn easier.[1] As stated in Chapter 1, the equation of exchange *per se* is an identity, not a theory. What makes it into a theory is the assertion, or claim, depending on one's normative conviction, that changes in the supply of money cause changes in the price level. Assuming this is true, the manipulation of the supply of money to change prices is known as monetary policy, that is, using money to achieve an economic or even political objective. In order to be able to conduct monetary or fiscal policy, it is necessary to have a theoretical link between the instrument and the economic outcome. The mere existence of an association such as the one between prices and the supply of money is not sufficient to merit its use as a policy instrument. For example, without doubt, the amount of rainfall has an impact on agricultural output and other economic realities. However, the government cannot manipulate the amount of rainfall to achieve a particular economic outcome like price stability. Monetary economists, observing the relationship between the supply of money and price levels, presumed two things. First, they assumed there is a causal relationship between the two, and second, that the causal relationship can be utilized effectively to achieve more desirable outcomes by changing the course of the economy. The effectiveness of monetary and fiscal policy is in fact at the heart of debate on the issue of which policy, if any, should be utilized.

Prior to Keynes,[2] economists did not advocate any particular economic role for the government in the economy. Governments were *de facto* facts of life and necessary to maintain law and order and fight foreign countries as needed. The mere existence of government means that government has expenditures and needs to collect taxes to pay for them. Neither the existence of government nor taxes are new. The control of foreign trade is another area in which governments have been involved for centuries. For example, the effect of government restriction of trade via imposition of tariffs was studied by classical economists, most notably by Ricardo.[3] The thing that was missing in these early approaches was the role of government intervention in the economy for the purpose of changing its course.

When is Government Intervention Permissible?

None of the classical economists wanted to abolish the government, which is the stated principle of the Nihilists. Smith[4] expects governments to enforce contracts, provide national security, perform public services, and to create and maintain infrastructure. The expectation that governments should perform certain tasks is not necessarily a gesture of good will. Governments are like double-edged swords. All taxes are contractionary and reduce the welfare of the tax-payers. On the other hand government expenditures provide income and hence utility for their recipients, not to mention public goods and services that are provided, such as roads. Furthermore, there are certain goods like national security, that benefit everyone, but they are not profitable enough for private enterprises to provide them. The reason they are not profitable is due to the nonexclusionary nature of such goods, which makes it impossible for market forces to allocate them efficiently, if at all.

Definition

Nonexclusion nature of public goods refers to the fact that once the good is provided everybody will benefit from it, even if they choose not to pay for it. A good example is national security.

Public goods are nonexhaustive, that is, their consumption by one person does not deprive someone else from using them as well. The beauty of a natural view does not vanish upon utilization by a person, although, too many visitors to a secluded area will destroy its seclusion. Another group of products that require government intervention in the market are goods with externalities.

Definition

Externalities are consequences, both positive and negative, that were not brought about by one's choice and action.

At the level of individuals, one might receive a positive externality from a neighbor's flower bed; a utility gain at zero cost. One might receive a negative externality from a neighbor's noisy party or construction. At the firm level, externalities are present in similar fashions. A classic example, dating to the early days of industrial revolution, is demonstrated by the smoke of a factory falling on clean laundry drying in the sun. Since the polluting factory does not have to pay for the cost of re-cleaning the laundry, it will overproduce the polluting good causing negative externalities. On the other hand, goods with positive externalities like education will be under-produced in a competitive market. In order for the society to produce the utility maximizing amount of education, it is necessary for the government to intervene in the economy in some fashion, such as subsidizing education or even supplying education.

There is no invisible hand that is capable of moving resources from one industry to another to maximize social welfare when externalities exist. It is beneficial to the society when the government facilitates the production of goods with positive externalities. One of the goods that Smith[5] believes should be provided by the government is education, which is a good with positive externalities. Educated people are more engaged in society and create more output than uneducated people. When people have to pay for the full cost of education they would demand less education than society would prefer. Governments help the production of education by direct payment to educational facilities, grants to students, subsidies, tax breaks and incentives, and issuance of bonds to construct buildings, to name a few.

Customarily, discussions of government intervention are not about national security, public education, and infrastructure. Among non-economists the discussion is mostly politically motivated and normative in nature. For example, people with a tendency to lean to the right politically advocate smaller government, while people at the center, or slightly to the left of center, petition for social justice and equality. People at the far left would rather replace the existing system with a socialist one.

These are the common political views of the 21st century in the United States, where few people remain at the far left in the United States.

Public discussions about government expenditures seem to be mostly about transfer payments. Democrats believe the income gap between the haves and have-nots is too wide and unemployed and low-income people are suffering; hence, income should be redistributed for greater social justice. Republicans, on the other hand, believe that transfer payments destroy the motivation to work and to be productive, at least for some recipients, while too much tax reduces the incentive to invest and create jobs. However, when the entire discussion is considered, it seems that both the Republicans and the Democrats demand a larger and a smaller government at the same time, although for different reasons. On one hand, while many Democrats favor less military expenditures, many also favor more assistance for the poor, unemployed, and orphans. On the other hand, while many Republicans favor greater military expenditures, many also favor less transfer payments. At times it seems that it is not the size of the government that is the real focus of the debate, rather it is the nature of government expenditures; thus revealing the normative nature of the discussion. From an economic perspective the magnitude of government expenditures is the relevant factor and most often the nature of these expenditures does not affect economic outcomes. A dollar given to a person as income is spent on goods and services, which becomes someone else's income. Every time the process is repeated GDP is increased by a fraction of the initial expenditure, regardless of whether it is for welfare or weapons system. This is a simplified version of the multiplier effect, which is the foundation of fiscal policy.[6]

Definition

Multiplier effect refers to the successive rounds of income consumption generated by an initial increase in consumption, investment, or government expenditures.

It is true that the multiplier effect is the same regardless of whether the initial expenditure is due to citizens' consumption, their investments, or government expenditures. However, this static approach fails to explain how the original dollar was obtained. For a consumer to spend a dollar on consumption or investment, he or she not only must have a dollar, but that dollar should also have not been earmarked for expenditures on something else in the first place.

The current level of GDP is the result of all the transactions that have already taken place. In order to increase GDP it is necessary to have new and additional expenditures. If a person is hiding cash in a mattress he or she can get it out, spend it, and increase GDP via the multiplier effect. When such extra cash is not available the economy cannot be stimulated.

Governments have a similar dilemma. In order to spend, the government must somehow obtain the money. Taxes generate revenue for the government to spend, but taxation takes money out of the hands of the citizens, thus reducing their expenditures.

Taking money away from economic agents sets the multiplier effect into motion, but this time in the opposite direction, causing a reduction in GDP. When the government spends taxes it creates new income via the same multiplier effect mechanism. There is no reason for the effects of the reduction and increase in income caused by the sequence of taxes and expenditures to be different. Therefore, there is no stimulating effect when government expenditures are generated through taxes. The statement is not valid if the marginal propensity to consume for citizens and the government are different. However, in order for fiscal policy to be effective, the government must inject new money into the economy. One alternative way of doing so is by deficit financing.[7]

Definition

Marginal propensity to consume is the percentage change in consumption due to a one percentage change in income.

Governments can also stimulate the economy using monetary instruments, which are covered in Chapter 3. Here, too, the choices are political. Should the government print more money, or should it buy bonds? The final economic aggregate outcome is the same in many aspects, but different segments of economy and different groups of people gain or lose and to varying extent, depending on how the monetary is implemented; a fact that was known in the 18th century.[8]

Economists are not able to determine the change in the total welfare of a society when money is transferred from one segment of society to another. For example, when the government issues bonds, the people who purchase the bonds receive dividends in the form of earned interest. The bonds and their interests must be paid through taxes that are levied on the entire population. Therefore, funds are transferred from taxpayers to bond holders. There is no mechanism in economics to compare the gain of utility by a millionaire as a consequence of receiving $100 interest on bonds to the loss of utility of losing the same $100 through taxes to pay the national debt. Economic theory can only ascertain that the utility of the former increases while that of the latter decreases. It is not possible, with the state of economic knowledge at our disposal, to determine which utility would be greater. Part of the problem is the inability to prove or disprove whether the utility of money decreases with increased ownership of money, a principle that applies to all other goods and services.

From a social perspective, taxes are not just a means for financing government expenditures, but they are also a way of improving social justice. The progressive taxes that are in effect in most countries, including the United States, are designed to reduce income and wealth differences in society. Progressive taxes are based on the notion of ability to bear the burden of taxes. It is noteworthy to point out that the term "progressive" in the progressive tax mechanism does not refer to the notion of enlightenment; rather, it alludes to the "increasing or graduated" notion of the term. An extreme case of this concept is the motto of communism: "From each according to his ability, to each according to his need."[9] For historical accuracy it is noteworthy that Blanc[10] used the phrase for the first time. Capitalists believe that adherence to this slogan would destroy incentives to work and produce and would cause economic, as well as social, decline.

In general, the political right in the United States prefers monetary policy to fiscal policy, even then, less government is preferred. This makes economic sense under a graduated income tax system. Under such systems higher-income people would pay a larger share of the tax burden, but receive less of its benefits. The requirement of smaller government seems to be a philosophical one at first. However, if a smaller government also implies less regulation due to the inability to enforce, then it would make sense for business owners to favor a smaller government. Government regulations increase production costs in many ways, the least of which is creating a paper trail demonstrating compliances with regulations. Such paper trails are deadweight loss to society. They cost to produce but some of their benefits are of dubious utility. Powerful governments are people's response to formidable and uncontrollable corporations, whose interest do not necessarily coincide with the majority of the population.

Definition

Deadweight loss is the loss of welfare as a result of government intervention or departures from resource allocation that would have prevailed under perfectly competitive markets for any reason, or by any means.

Some regulations increase production costs due to the necessity of using less productive methods. For example, in order to comply with pollution standards it is necessary to use more expensive fuel, filters, and cleanup procedures. Note that these requirements not only increase production costs for producers, but also increase social welfare. The increase in social welfare is bestowed upon all citizens regardless of participation or payment. This nonexclusion means that producers of goods cannot charge more for producing the same good by a cleaner method, so they bear the cost, but not the benefit. This is an example where government intervention is acceptable for classical economists. It is important to note that part of the increase in production costs caused by regulations can be transferred to the consumers of the good. The extent of the transfer of the burden depends on the elasticity of demand and supply functions.

Political Case against Monetary Policy

There is little argument against monetary policy, be it economic or political. The fiscalists, especially during the latter part of the 20th century, have come to accept that monetary instruments are powerful tools that can and should be utilized when the economic situation is not desirable. In fact, since the 1980s the majority of government intervention in the economy has been through monetary policy, rather than fiscal policy. However, during recessionary periods, especially when the interest rate is pushed down toward zero, monetary policy instruments become dull and lose their power; hence fiscal policy becomes more effective.

Keynes[11] developed the fiscal theory during the Great Depression, when monetary policy became utterly ineffective. It is also possible that the monetary authorities of the time made the wrong decisions and employed inappropriate monetary tools.

Ironically, the main opposition to the use of monetary policy belongs to monetary theorists, especially Friedman. Friedman's opposition to the use of monetary policy is not philosophical or due to ineffectiveness of monetary instruments. His concern is based on two reasons. The first reason for the opposition is pragmatic, and the second one is because monetary instruments are potent. Friedman[12] has no doubt that monetary instruments are more effective than fiscal instruments; therefore, monetary policy is better than fiscal policy. Nevertheless, he argues that there are two types of lags that make the use of monetary policy problematic. One set of lags is generated in the time it takes to select and implement policy instruments and the other set between implementing monetary tools and the time it takes for them to change the course of the economy. These are called, respectively, inside and outside lags.

Definition

An **inside lag** is the time between recognition of the need for a stimulus or restrain and the legislation of the appropriate regulations.

Definition

An **outside lag** is the time between a policy action and the appearance of its effects in the economy.

Friedman and Schwarz[13] obtain long and irregular lags indicating the difficulty in pinpointing their full effects. They draw attention to the possibility that by the time the full effect materializes the economy is in a different state. It is possible that by the time a remedy for a recession begins working the economy is already out of recession, and the added stimulate could result in inflation. Friedman also argues that since the state of statistical analysis is not advanced enough to identify the correct position of the economy on a business cycle, the decision of prescribing a solution is based on incomplete and inaccurate information. Consequently, he recommends increasing the supply of money by a fixed rate to match the long run economic trend and expansion to accommodate increased (average) growth rates in GDP and population. This idea is the basis of the analysis of "rules versus authorities" by Simons.[14] Later, the rational expectations hypothesis provided another dimension to the debate by demonstrating that only unexpected fiscal and monetary shocks can have economic impacts, and then, only in the short run.[15]

Friedman's[16] suggestion that the money supply should increase at a constant rate that reflects the trends in economic and population growth is also problematic since it ignores economic reality and ties down the hands of the authorities. Taylor[17] proposes a compromise in the form of an inflation targeting rule. Inflation targeting takes advantage of the rational expectations hypothesis that setting and diligently following a stated policy would reduce uncertainty in the market and increase information, thus allowing economic agents to make informed decisions. This type of policy reduces the cost of obtaining information and increases the ability of economic agents to predict the outcome of economic activities, as set forth by the rational expectations hypothesis. Inflation targeting also takes advantage of having a rule, albeit broadly interpreted, by allowing the central bank to examine trends and to make monetary decisions for the long run. Since 1993, several countries have officially adopted an inflation targeting policy, where their respective central banks have declared inflation targets based on their country's long run economic trends. The results have been a substantial decline in inflation rates around the globe, most notably in Latin America. The United States has not declared an inflation targeting policy; however, the original Taylor Rule was defined on the basis of U.S. data and according to Goodfriend,[18] the Federal Reserve has been pursuing such a policy since post–World War II era.

CHAPTER 3

Two Blades are Better than One: The Role of IS-LM

IS–LM analysis is an important tool that acknowledges the fact that for equilibrium to prevail in an economy it is necessary to have equilibrium in both the goods and the money markets simultaneously. To avoid undue complexity, equilibrium in each market is presented separately and then combined for the final analysis. Both markets rely on the interest rate to provide necessary signals for investment and lending decisions.

Definition

The **IS schedule** is the loci of interest rate-output sets for which the goods market is in equilibrium.

Definition

The **LM schedule** is the loci of combinations of interest rates and incomes that result in equilibrium in the money market.

Aggregate Demand

For derivation of IS schedule it is necessary to define aggregate demand in the goods market, which represents total production. Aggregate demand consists of the sum of individual **consumption** (C) **investment** (I) by firms plus government **expenditures** (G) and **foreign trade**. Foreign trade consists of two components, **imports** (M) and **exports** (X). Customarily, **net trade** is utilized ($X - M$) and is represented by NX in the following equation. Therefore, aggregate demand (Y) is the sum of all demands by all sectors

$$Y = C + I + G + NX \qquad (3.1)$$

In static equilibrium the process of moving from one equilibrium point to another is ignored, while various measures are compared. For example, in order to increase the government's expenditures either taxes or debt must be increased. In a static comparative analysis the consequences of such increases are ignored and attention is focused on the effect of the increase in government expenditures on aggregate demand. In a dynamic study, consequences of the need to increase taxes or the national debt are incorporated, and the feedback of the resulting consequences of such increases is integrated into the model to provide a more realistic outcome. Customarily, static models are used for ease of presentation; a practice that will be pursued here.

Equations, such as 3.1, do not provide any information about the nature of each variable and how they are determined. It is possible to assume that all the components on the right-hand side are determined without regard to economic conditions; in other words, they are exogenous variables. This is a common practice in elementary economics. Initially, all variables except consumption are assumed to be exogenous to demonstrate the effect of changes in aggregate demand on income. Consumption is stated as a function of income; a fact that is implied by the MPC. In the presence of taxes and **transfer payments** (TP), consumption is a function of disposable income instead of income. More realistically, each variable can be expressed in terms of the factors that influence it.

Definition

Disposable income is gross income minus taxes plus transfer payments.

Recall that "aggregate income," by definition, is equal to "aggregate output." For the sake of brevity, the word "aggregate" is omitted when there is no ambiguity. It can be shown[1] that when investment and taxes are determined endogenously through links to interest rate and income, respectively, the multiplier effect is obtained by equation 3.2.

$$Y = \frac{C_0 + cTP_0 + I_0 + G_0}{1 - c(1 - t)} - \frac{b}{1 - c(1 - t)}i \qquad (3.2)$$

where c is the MPC, t the tax rate, b the responsiveness of investment to changes in the interest rate, and i the interest rate. The terms that appear in the numerator of the first part are the constant terms representing the autonomous components of consumption, transfer payments, investment, and government expenditures, respectively. Changes in the constants of the model result in shifts in aggregate demand, while changes in the parameters of the model, namely c, t, and b, cause changes in the slope of aggregate demand; hence the magnitude of the multiplier effect.

Equation 3.2 is useful in explaining the IS schedule as well as the multiplier effect. Equation 3.2 presents the multiplier effect of a change in the interest rate on income, assuming everything else remains the same.

Multiplier Effect

Let one of the factors that are constant change from state zero to state one. Factors that affect constants are exogenous, that is, they are not influenced by economic forces; instead they change due to noneconomic causes like changes in taste. For example, suppose government expenditures changes from G_0 to G_1. In state zero, output is Y_0, shown in equation 3.3, and in state one it is Y_1, shown in equation 3.4.

$$Y_0 = \frac{C_0 - cT_0 + cTP_0 + I_0 + G_0}{1 - c(1-t)} - \frac{b}{1 - c(1-t)}i \qquad (3.3)$$

$$Y_1 = \frac{C_0 - cT_0 + cTP_0 + I_0 + G_1}{1 - c(1-t)} - \frac{b}{1 - c(1-t)}i \qquad (3.4)$$

The difference in the two states is the change in output in response to changes in government expenditures.

$$Y_1 - Y_0 = \frac{1}{1 - c(1-t)}(G_1 - G_0) \qquad (3.5)$$

The magnitude $k = \frac{1}{1 - c(1-t)}$ is the multiplier effect. Since both c and t are between zero and one the magnitude of k is greater than one.

Balanced Budget Multiplier

In the above example, government expenditures increase, as if by magic. In real life, the increase must be funded in some way. One possibility is to fund government expenditures through deficit financing. An alternative way is to increase taxes to equal the increase in expenditure. The multiplier in the case of deficit financing is the same as described above. When taxes are increased to pay for the additional government expenditures the government is using a balanced budget on new expenditures; therefore both G and T must change by equal amounts. Assuming that the government increases the exogenous portion of the taxes without increasing the tax rate equation 3.6 becomes:

$$Y_1 - Y_0 = \frac{1}{1 - c(1-t)}(G_1 - G_0) - \frac{c}{1 - c(1-t)}(T_1 - T_0) \qquad (3.6)$$

Since the increase in expenditures is equal to the increase in taxes $(G_1 - G_0) = (T_1 - T_0)$ the multiplier is:

$$k = \frac{1-c}{1 - c(1-b)} \qquad (3.7)$$

The multiplier effect is much smaller when balanced budget is used instead of deficit financing. Figure 3.1 provides a visual presentation of the change in income as a result of a change in government expenditures. A change in government expenditures by the magnitude of $(G_1 - G_0)$ shifts aggregate expenditure up from $C + I + G_0$ to $C + I + G_1$. As a result income increases from Y_0 to Y_1.

As a result of a change in G the economy is jolted out of its initial equilibrium point of E_0 toward point A. Since, at point A, the economy is not at equilibrium there is excess demand pressuring output to increase toward point B. The mechanism by which this occurs is through price changes. As a result of the increase in output income increases proportionately to the MPC, causing the economy to move in the direction of point C. The cycle repeats and the economy moves toward point D, until the economy reaches the new equilibrium point E_1. Note that at each successive round the increase in income and the pursuing consumption becomes smaller.

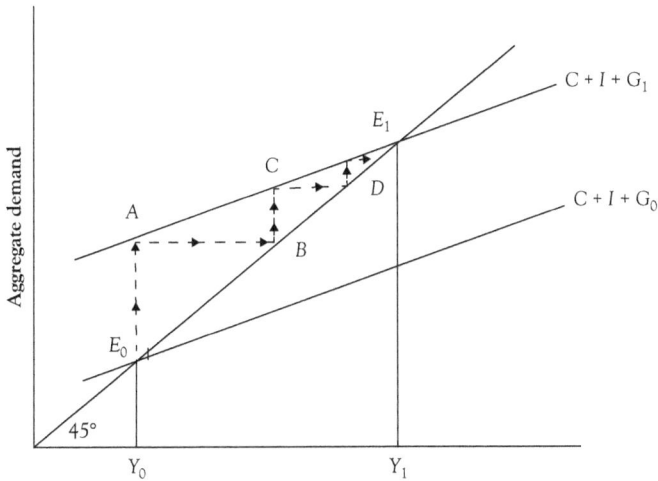

Figure 3.1 Changes in output as a result of a shift in government expenditures

IS Schedule

The starting point for deriving the IS schedule is the endogenous investment function of equation 3.8, which relates investment to the interest rate.

$$I = I_0 + bY \tag{3.8}$$

The relationship between investment and the interest rate is believed to be inverse, which is represented by a negative sign in front of coefficient b; the responsiveness of investment to the interest rate. Figure 3.2 depicts the investment function. Technically, the equation represents firms' planned investment. However, at equilibrium, planned and actual investments are equal.

As is evident in panel A of Figure 3.2, a decrease in interest rate from i_0 to i_1 will cause an increase in investment from I_0 to I_1. However, an increase in investment will shift aggregate demand upward from $C + I_0 + G$ to $C + I_1 + G$, which results in an increase in income or output from Y_0 to Y_1, as shown in panel B of Figure 3.2.

The change in the interest rate also affects savings. Since whatever is not consumed is saved implies:

$$S = -C_0 + (1 - \text{MPC})Y \tag{3.9}$$

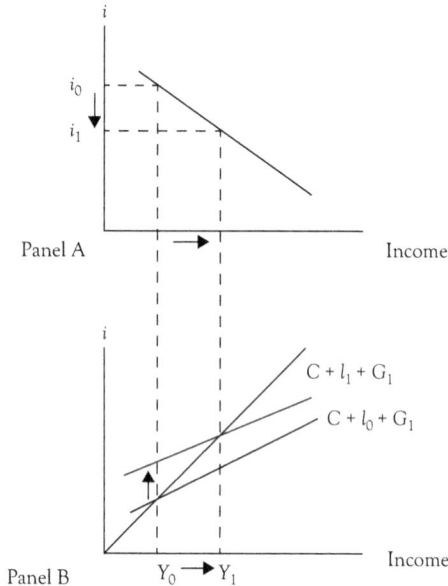

Figure 3.2 *Investment function*

Since savings must be equal to investment at equilibrium, the change in investment due to a change in the interest rate can be transferred to the savings function. Figure 3.3 depicts the top part of Figure 3.2 in panel A. Panel B of the graph simply transfers the changes in investment to their equivalent changes in savings in panel C. This takes places via the equilibrium condition of $I = S$ in panel B, which is simply the 45-degree line that transfers movements along the investment line to that of the savings line. Panel C provides the link between saving and income. From panel A, it is possible to track how a change in the interest rate elicits changes in investment that can be tracked to panel D to find changes in income. Assuming all other factors remain constant in the goods market, the change in investment is the only factor that affects output. Transferring the two interest rates i_0 and i_1 from panel A to panel D provides the necessary information about the interest rate, needed to determine the change in income. Transmitting the two incomes from panel C to panel D provides information about income. The intersection of these two sets of information provides two points in the interest–income plane in panel D. The resulting IS schedule is the loci of equilibrium points in the goods market for different levels of interest rates.

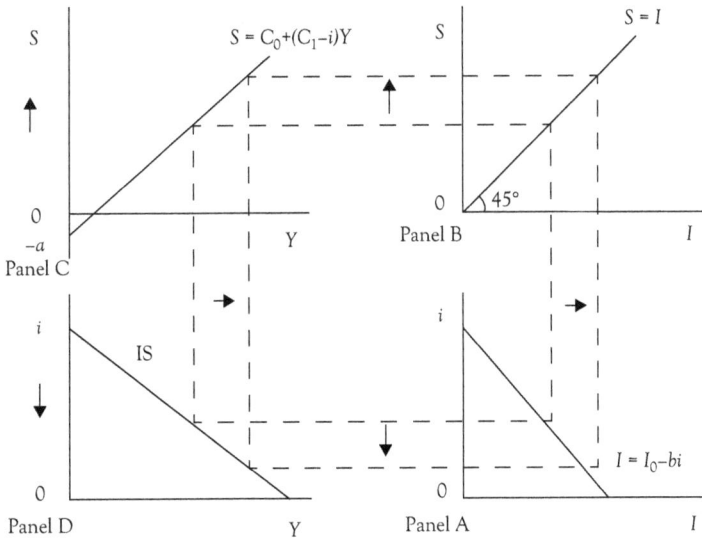

Figure 3.3 Derivation of the IS schedule

The magnitude of the change in income in panel D of Figure 3.3 is the same as the shift in panel B of Figure 3.2.

LM Schedule

The demand for money is a function of two variables, which are the interest rate and income level. In order to isolate the effect of the interest rate, we allow income levels to change as in the left panel of Figure 3.4 and trace the effect of the change in the right panel of Figure 3.4 to obtain the LM schedule. The two lines in the left panel correspond to two different levels of income, Y_1 and Y_2. Since the left panel does not represent income on either axis, a change in Y from lower value, Y_1, to higher value, Y_2, causes an upward shift in the line.

The LM schedule shows the relationship between income and the interest rate. When the interest rate increases, the opportunity cost of money increases; therefore, the demand for money declines. Since the supply of money is inelastic and remains constant, the money market will be out of equilibrium. In order for the demand for money to increase to the (previous) equilibrium level, it is necessary for income to increase, which causes an increase in the demand for money. Consequently, depicting the

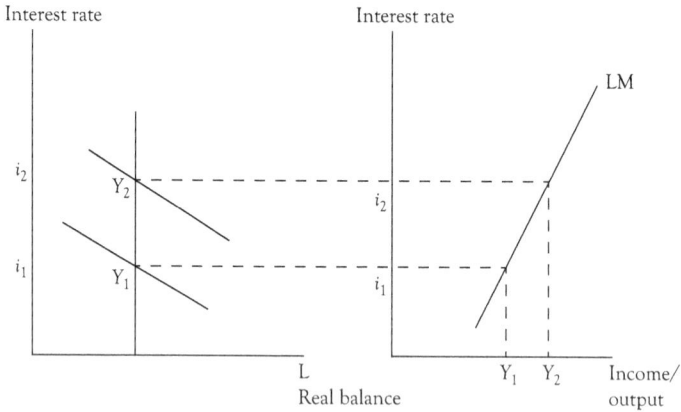

Figure 3.4 Derivation of the LM schedule

relationship between the interest rate and income in first graph would indicate that the result of an increase in the interest rate is an increase in income. Therefore, the LM schedule is an upward sloping curve.

Equilibrium in the Goods and Money Market

The IS schedule depicts the points along which pairs of interest rates and income levels result in equilibrium in the goods market. The LM schedule depicts the points along which pairs of the interest rate and income are at equilibrium in the money market. Combining these, as in Figure 3.5, provides the unique combination of the level of income and interest rate at which both the goods and money markets are at equilibrium. This corresponds to the intersection of the two curves, which is similar to the intersection of supply and demand in a single market case.

In order to determine the derivations of the IS and LM schedules, we made the simplifying assumption of constant prices and the ability of producers to increase their output without the need for a price increase. These assumptions are usually the characteristics of an underemployed and underutilized economy, which prevails during a recessionary period. Technically, except for when the economy is at full employment, there is always excess capacity. There is excess capacity when an economy slows down, when it is in recession, and during recovery.

The essence of proponents' arguments for both fiscal and monetary policy is based on the slopes of the IS and LM curves and what

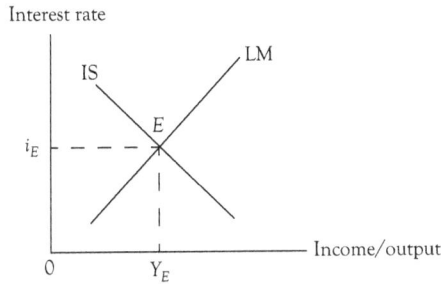

Figure 3.5 IS–LM schedule and market equilibrium

happens when one or the other shifts. The present book discusses the impact of changes in economic variables from the perspective of monetary policy.

Effectiveness of Fiscal and Monetary Policies

The effectiveness of fiscal and monetary policies depends on the slopes of the IS and LM curves. The IS schedule is downward sloping which indicates that a decrease in the interest rate will increase investment, and as a result, output, through:

$$Y = C + I + G + (M - X)$$

Since the interest rate is not represented on either axis of the aggregate demand-aggregate supply diagram, the result of a change in the interest rate appears as an upward shift in aggregate demand. At the new equilibrium, output will be higher as well to match the increased demand. Equation 3.8 indicates that a change in the interest rate changes I, which in turn, through equation 3.1, changes output. This change is a movement along the IS curve. Output can also change due to change in the magnitude of any of the constant factors grouped together in the first part of the equation 3.3. A change in these variables would cause a shift in the IS schedule.

An Increase in Government Expenditures

The advocates of fiscal policy point out that an increase in the government expenditure would shift the IS curve to the right and increase

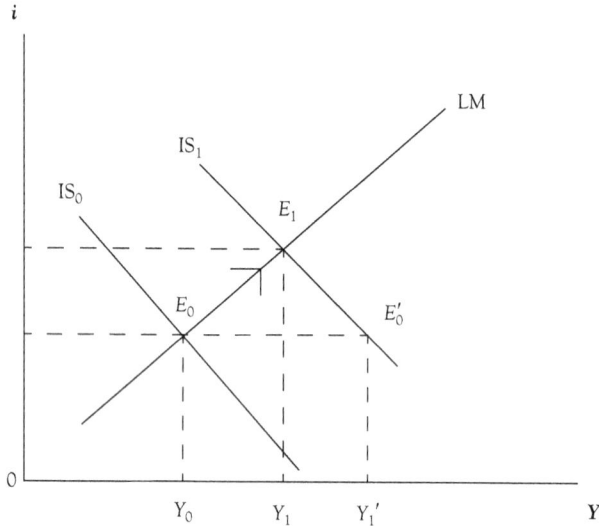

Figure 3.6 Effect of an increase in government expenditure

output. Starting at the equilibrium point of E_0 in Figure 3.6 the shift in IS increases output from Y_0 to Y_1'. However, this static analysis is not complete. The result of the increase in output is that the money market is not at equilibrium and point E_0' is not sustainable. The increased income increases the demand for money, which exerts an upward pressure on the interest rate. The increase in income increases the demand for money, which causes the interest rate to increase. A decrease in investment and consumption causes a reduction in income until both the goods and money market are at equilibrium at point E_1.

Definition

Crowding Out refers to an increase in interest rate as a result of expansionary fiscal policy.

Classical Economics and Crowding Out

Crowding out occurs as a result of an increase in investment in response to an increased demand for goods, which resulted from an increase in government expenditures. However, it is not clear how crowding out could exist during recessionary periods when there is idle capacity and output can increase without pressure on prices.

Unless the Fed accommodates the expansionary fiscal policy with easy money policy the increase in output will be Y_1, which is less than Y_1'. In order for an increase in output to materialize it is necessary for the LM schedule not to be perfectly inelastic; as claimed by the classical economists.

Classical economists argue that the demand for money is determined by the value of transactions (QP) and not affected by the interest rate. Consequently, demand for money is interest inelastic and the LM schedule is vertical. Under this condition an increase in government expenditures only increases the interest rate, which causes enough reduction in investment to offset the expansionary effect of government expenditures without any increase in output or income, as depicted in Figure 3.7.

When the LM schedule is not perfectly inelastic with respect to the interest rate, the extent of the effectiveness of an expansionary fiscal policy depends on the slope of the LM curve, other things equal, which in turn is a function of the interest rate elasticity of the demand for money.

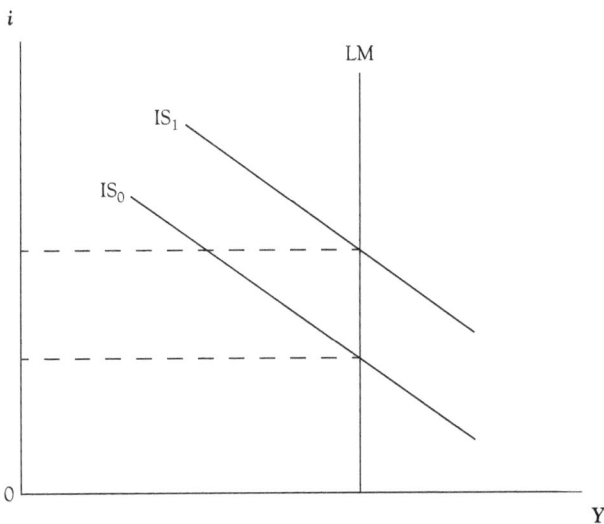

Figure 3.7 *Vertical LM and ineffectiveness of fiscal policy* (crowding out)

Liquidity Trap and Fiscal Policy

The opposite of the effectiveness of a vertical LM is a horizontal one. A horizontal LM curve is the situation in which the change in the supply of money is incapable of changing the interest rate, which is also called a liquidity trap. In the presence of a liquidity trap the demand for money is perfectly elastic, which translates into a horizontal LM curve. When interest rates are low enough to create a liquidity trap an expansion in government expenditures does not cause an increase in the interest rate. Therefore, crowding out does not occur, and fiscal policy is more effective, while monetary policy is completely ineffective. The policy implication is that government stimuli are at their full potential when there is liquidity trap and the interest rate is very low, such as during a recession. The presence of a liquidity trap makes the impact of fiscal policy stronger regardless of whether government expenditures are increased or decreased. Therefore, expenditure cuts during a recession would be detrimental to the economy. Figure 3.8 depicts the effect of an increase in government expenditures in the presence of liquidity trap.

The existence of liquidity trap must be accompanied with two other conditions for the above argument to be valid. First, investment must

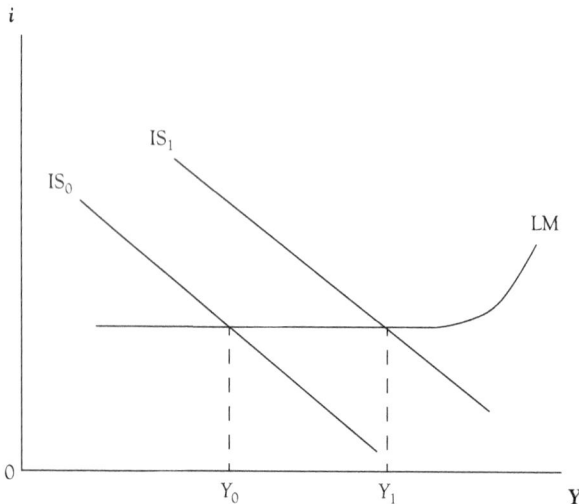

Figure 3.8 Horizontal LM and maximum effectiveness of fiscal policy (liquidity trap)

have low interest elasticity. Therefore, lower interest rates hardly result in an increase in investment. Second, labor should prefer to be unemployed than accept lower wages. Resistance of wages to decline is sometimes called sticky wages.

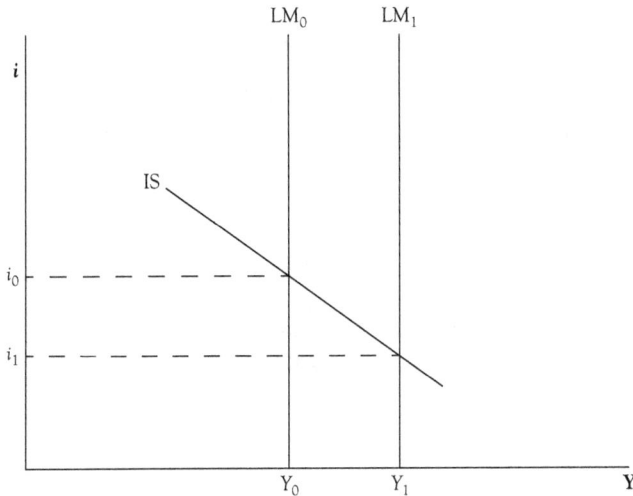

Figure 3.9 Vertical LM and effectiveness of monetary policy

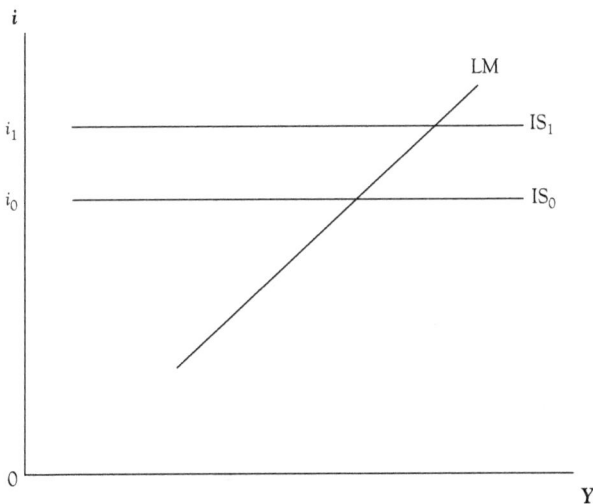

Figure 3.10 Horizontal IS and effectiveness of monetary policy

Earlier it was said that the assumptions of the classical economics makes the LM schedule vertical. A vertical LM makes fiscal policy ineffective, while making monetary policy very effective. An expansionary monetary policy when the LM is vertical not only increases output but also reduces the interest rate.

Horizontal IS

A horizontal IS indicates fiscal policy will be ineffective, while monetary policy remains effective. Figure 3.10 presents such a scenario. As the slope of the LM curve increases its effectiveness also increases.

Vertical LM and Horizontal IS

The ultimate effectiveness of monetary policy occurs when the LM schedule is vertical and the IS schedule is horizontal, simultaneously. Under these conditions, the maximum effectiveness of monetary policy is combined with utterly ineffective fiscal policy, which is depicted in Figure 3.11.

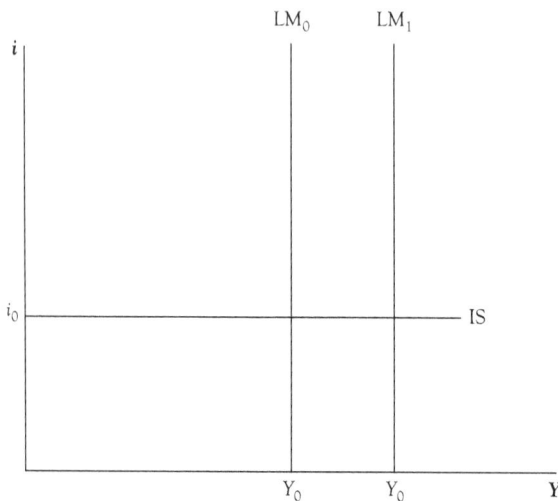

Figure 3.11 Vertical LM and horizontal IS

CHAPTER 4

The Role of Velocity in Monetary Policy

The first prominent view on the role of money in the economy was Fisher's[1] formulation of the quantity theory of money, explained in Chapter 1 and presented in equation 1.1, which is repeated here for reference.

$$MV \equiv PQ \qquad (4.1)$$

where V is the velocity of money (M), which is assumed to be fairly stable over time for a given economy, P is the price level or average prices, and Q is the output of the economy, in a closed economy. At least as early as the 18th century, economists realized that the value of transactions in an economy far exceeds the physical supply of money, which, until 1971, was mostly metal based in some fashion. The only logical explanation for this possibility is that money changes hands more than once in the course of a year. It seems that in order to verify equation 4.1, it is necessary to measure velocity directly, but since the equation is just an identity it suffices to know the value of all transactions in a year, or GDP. However, GDP was calculated for the first time by Kuznets in 1934.[2] In spite of the fact that concepts of GDP were more theoretical than observational until 1934, classical economists also postulate that velocity is constant. This assumption is a foundation of the early quantity theory of demand for money and monetary theory. Twentieth-century economists, including advocates of both fiscal and monetary policy, agree that the velocity of money is fairly stable and changes only gradually. The reason early economists assumed velocity is constant is because it depends on economic and social institutions, which in turn change gradually, as will be explained in Chapter 6.

Institutional Factors Affecting Velocity

The more frequently money is exchanged the faster velocity is. Velocity is high in an economy in which everybody is paid each day, which requires less money than economies with less-frequent wage payments. As the frequency of pay decreases from daily to weekly, or monthly periods, the demand for money for transaction purposes increases and its velocity decreases. It can be shown that under some simplistic and reasonably realistic assumptions the amount of cash necessary over the course of any given period is obtained by:

$$M = \sqrt{\frac{2cY}{i}}$$

(4.2)

where M is cash holding per period, c is transaction cost, Y is income per period, and i is the interest rate of the asset.[3] The transaction demand for money is a fraction of the demand for money and depends on the income level. At low income levels most of one's income is used for consumption, which is the main part of transaction demand for money. As income increases, it is possible to save some of it due to other motives, such as the precautionary or speculative motives.[4]

Equation 4.1 presents the demand for money as the square root of transaction costs, income, and the interest rate. Transaction costs are the costs of converting interest-bearing assets to cash. However, electronic advancements have reduced the cost of transactions, or the transfer of money. Therefore, more income can be kept in interest-bearing assets and the velocity of money increases. The equation indicates that an increase in income (Y) will increase the demand for money (M), but only by the square root of the increase in income. In order for the demand for money for transaction purposes to double, income must quadruple, other things equal. Most demand for money functions, such as Baumol's,[5] relate the demand for money to the interest rate, while quantity theory only links money to the value of all transactions. The argument here is that as the interest rate increases, the opportunity cost of holding money increases; thus, it becomes worthwhile to hold less money and more interest-bearing assets in order to earn more revenue.

Here, too, the relationship is based on the square root. In order for the demand for money to double the interest rate must decrease by four times. However, the range of possible interest rates is limited. Although theoretically it is possible to have a negative nominal interest rate, such as during high and unexpected inflations, the lower bound of nominal interest rates should remain positive in order to induce investment. Historically, real interest rates, even in countries with limited capital, have been less than 20%. The discussion here is limited to the base interest rate for a risk free asset, such as the U.S. Treasury Bond. Exorbitant interest rates exist because of higher risk.

It is suggested that the real interest rate in the United States is around 4%. According to equation 4.2, in order to reduce the demand for money for transaction purposes by half, the interest rate must increase to 16%. However, three factors limit the effect of the interest rate on the demand for money. First, there is a limited range of values for the interest rate. Second, the relationship between money demand and interest rate is in square root form. Third, the stated relationship is for the transaction demand for money, which is only one component of the overall demand for money. The actual real interest rates are more compact and range between -1.47% (1975) and 8.68% (1981). Figure 4.1 depicts real interest rates for the United States between 1961 and 2010.

Logic would imply that the greater the supply of money in circulation, the less its velocity would be. However, early economists argued that an

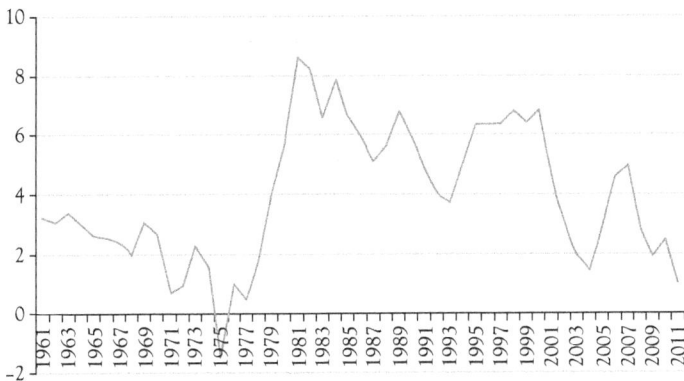

Figure 4.1 Interest rates for United States 1961–2010

Source: World Bank development indicators.

increase in the supply of money would increase prices rather than reduce velocity. Therefore, the assumption is that the velocity of money is not sensitive to changes in the supply of money. Thus, two major shortcomings of classical economics are the lack of association between the supply of money and its velocity, and the insensitivity of the demand for money to changes in the interest rate. These are not trivial issues. The implication of constant velocity is that an increase in the supply of money must either increase output or prices. Since the production function determines output and is a function of natural resources, human capital, and institutions, such as the rule of law, output does not depend on the supply of money and cannot be changed. Thus, classical economists argue that the only variable that can increase in the short run is the price level.

Keynes,[6] on the other hand, linked the demand for money to the interest rate, which became accepted as orthodoxy to the point that monetary theorists like Friedman[7] began formulating the demand for money in terms of the interest rate, among other variables. Inclusion of the interest rate in the demand for money function leads to the derivation of the LM schedule. Classical economists claim that the demand for money is not a function of interest rate, which indicates that the elasticity of the demand for money with respect to the interest rate is zero. This implies a vertical LM curve. As discussed in Chapter 3, a vertical LM curve means that monetary policy is very effective and that fiscal policy is ineffective, irrespective of its slope. The idea of a perfectly inelastic demand for money is no longer supported by many economists. However, there is little evidence, maybe with the exception of severe recessions, to support the assumption of a perfectly elastic demand for money, either. The question of a perfectly inelastic versus perfectly elastic demand has become an empirical issue, with the matter of the degree of responsiveness of the demand for money to the interest rate being the subject of debate today. Numerous studies provide income elasticity of money for both M_1 and M_2, such as Stock and Watson,[8] Ball,[9] Alvarez and Lippi,[10] and Weeks.[11]

Velocity and Interest Rate

In Chapter 3 we did not provide an algebraic derivation for the LM schedule. It is customary in monetary theory to modify the equation of exchange to express it in terms of velocity. Before tending to that matter, let us provide a demand for money function in terms of the interest rate and output.

$$M/P = L\ (i,\ Y) \tag{4.3}$$

where M is the nominal demand for money, P is price level, i is the interest rate, and Y is output. Dividing nominal money by the price level provides the demand for real money as compared to nominal demand. The function simply expresses the demand for real money in terms of a non-specific function of the interest rate and output or income. There is no need to choose a specific functional form. It suffices to have an inverse relationship between the interest rate and the demand for real balances and a direct relationship between output or income and the demand for real money; a task that can be accomplished by requiring a negative sign in front of the interest rate in any specific model.

Rewriting equation 1.1, the equation of exchange, from Chapter 1 in terms of velocity:

$$V \equiv \frac{PY}{M} = \frac{Y}{M/P} \tag{4.4}$$

That is, velocity is equal to the ratio of real income to real balances. Since velocity is a function of real balances and income, and real balances is a function of the interest rate and income, equation 4.3 can be rewritten as:

$$V = \frac{1}{l(i)} \tag{4.5}$$

where $l(i)$ is some function of interest rate. Therefore, the modern quantity theory expresses velocity in terms of the interest rate. Figure 4.2 provides the relationship between velocity and the interest rate.

Under the modern quantity theory it is not necessary to assume that the velocity of money is constant. Nor is it necessary to assume full employment. Early monetarists misunderstood how velocity could

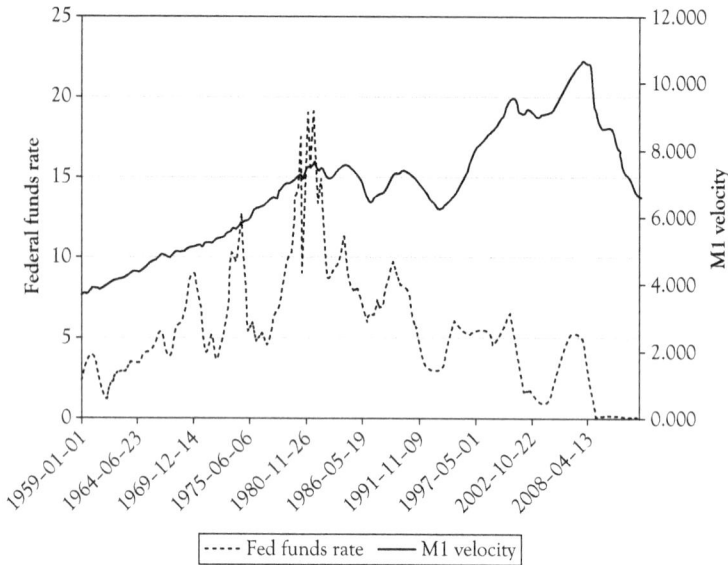

Figure 4.2 Velocity of money and interest rate
Source: Federal Reserve Bank of St. Louis (2013).

change with respect to income. For example, at high enough incomes, after all the supply of money has been allocated among its alternative uses and no idle cash is available, any additional income that is not matched by an increase in the supply of money would cause an increase in velocity in order to accommodate the economy.

Neither Fisher[12] nor other economists using the equation of exchange provided a direct way of estimating velocity. In fact, until the system of national accounting was established[13] there were no calculations made to obtain the value of all goods and services produced in the economy, that is, the right-hand side of the equation of exchange, which in turn is divided by the supply of money to estimate the velocity. Bruner and Meltzer[14] use adjustments to wealth to explain the demand for money similar to the portfolio balance approach. In this approach they express the demand for money as a function of the stock of wealth and the elasticity of demand for money with respect to the interest rate. They derive an approximation for velocity, which depends on both the price level and the supply of money. They use this estimated velocity to obtain an estimate of output with reasonable accuracy.

Other Factors Affecting Velocity

There are other factors that affect velocity, some more directly than others. As demonstrated earlier, an increase in income increases the demand for money. When the increased demand is not met by an equal increase in supply, velocity has to change, in order to avoid an economic bottleneck. Since the volume of transactions changes constantly so does the demand for money, which makes it almost impossible to match the demand for money with the supply of money. The link between the frequency of payment and the demand for money was also explained earlier. A change in quantity of money demanded changes its velocity. Finally, changes in the interest rate were shown to affect the demand for money and hence its velocity. Any factor that can affect one or more of these variables will also affect the velocity. Information about interest rates, the availability of bargains, cost of information, and risk also affects velocity. In turn, changes in velocity affect the slope of the LM curve, and hence the effectiveness of monetary policy.

SECTION II

Monetary Theory and Related Issues

CHAPTER 5

Keynes' View of Monetary Policy

Without doubt, the existence of a central bank is the most prominent symbol of the importance of monetary policy. The first central banks, Riksbank of Sweden, established in 1668 and the Bank of England that opened its doors in 1694, were privately owned and created to lend money to the government. In modern economies central banks are the ultimate monetary authority of their respective governments. Although the concept of a government-operated central bank with legislative authority to regulate the banking system, monetary system, monetary policy, and currency is well established now, that was not the case in the early 20th century. A misconception about Keynes is that he advocates the use of fiscal policy and believes monetary policy is ineffective. Keynes advocates that to end a money market crisis it is important for a government to act as the lender of last resort when there is no private central bank. An example of such a case is India at the end of the 19th century, which Keynes supported; he was the director of Bank of England as well.

On one hand, a central bank can maintain government and private reserves for times of need. However, central banks can go beyond this, and in practice they all do, by providing policies for the nation's banks and enforcing regulations to safeguard the monetary system from extreme fluctuations. On the other hand, as recently as 2013, some have questioned the wisdom of an independent and seemingly unaccountable central bank (for recent work on this matter, see works by Epstein[1] and Bernanke[2]). An independent central bank would be shielded from government interference and retain the power to make decisions for the economic welfare of the nation; however, complete independence could also be interpreted as, or lead to, a lack of accountability. History has shown that when a political party that controls one of the houses of a parliamentary-based system does not like the economic policies of its central bank, it calls for more control of the bank. Keynes[3] favors a central bank with discretionary power because he believes it is impossible to mimic "wise behavior" through rules and regulations.

Classical View of Money

The main premise of classical economics is based on the equation of exchange and holds that a change in the supply of money only affects the price level, and not output. This idea stems from the view that output is a function of economic, social, and political institutions, and depends on the production means of labor and capital under a given state of technology. Technology is believed to be exogenous to the economic system. The conclusion is that **money does not matter** with regard to production and economic growth. This detachment between the supply of money and the means of production is still believed to be true for the long run, where the fundamental characteristics of a nation determine its economic growth. The factors that influence long run output include human capital, the banking system, and types and magnitude of investment, to name a few.

Keynes' View of Money

The main focus of Keynes was on the issue of a liquidity trap during recession. As explained in detail earlier, when the interest rate is sufficiently low, an increase in the money supply cannot lower it further, therefore rendering monetary policy ineffective. This view prevailed for a long time. However, there is no evidence that Keynes, or early Keynesians, claimed monetary policy is ineffective. Nothing demonstrates this better than a popular statement of the era that monetary policy is like a string; one can pull it, but cannot push it. The implication is that like a string, monetary policy can pull the economy back from inflation and overproduction, but cannot push the economy out of recession, at least in part, due to the presence of a liquidity trap. Therefore, the proposition about the ineffectiveness of monetary policy is limited to the specific case of a serious depression and requires the presence of liquidity trap. This falls far short of stating that monetary policy is completely ineffective under all conditions and for any purposes. Keynes[4] refers to the monetary theory's equation of exchange to provide a plausible explanation for the lack of monetary policy's effectiveness with regard to expansionary power. From the equation of exchange, it is evident that an increase in supply of money can be offset by a decrease in velocity, a possibility that the classical economists did not acknowledge.

The following statement from the General Theory should clarify Keynes' view on the effectiveness of changing the money supply and hence, monetary theory. "So long as there is unemployment, employment will change in the same proportion as the quantity of money, and when there is full employment, prices will change in the same proportion as the quantity of money." The second part of the sentence is identical to the views of classical economists and implies **money does not matter**. However, the first part is a testament to the effectiveness of monetary policy and the belief that **money does matter**. In some cases, at least in his early writings, Keynes agrees with the classical economists that money does not matter.

Thus, the importance of fiscal policy is not because monetary policy is ineffective, but because it is ineffective in deep recessions and depressions. Under such conditions Keynes proposes an active role for government. He goes further by advocating discretionary policy, both fiscal and monetary. Soon after the *General Theory*, discretionary policy became prominent. Historically speaking, Kahn[5] introduced the possibility of discretionary fiscal policy and deserves the credit.

Definition

Discretionary policy refers to active government intervention in economic matters via fiscal policy, monetary policy, or both.

In time, Keynesian views were received with broader acceptance. Nevertheless, fiscal policy did not become an official policy of the U.S. government until the 1960s. Although both Keynes and the majority of his followers agree that monetary policy is effective and easy money policies reduce the interest rate, economists' early debates on the effectiveness of discretionary policy focused on comparisons of the relative efficacy of fiscal and monetary policies. Part of this discussion involves the issue of whether money matters or does not matter. Monetary theorists, in the tradition of the classical economists, argue that money does not matter.

Keynesians advocate that money does matter. At least the hardliners of each camp take this stance, perhaps for the sake of discussion and debate. Over time the monetarist camp took a harder line on the subject, while Keynesians took a more moderate stand and stated that money matters to some extent. Heller, for example, changed the question to "does money matter much."[6] Note that the statement "money does not matter" refers to the influence of changes in the supply of money on real output.

Friedman's View of Money

According to Friedman, the question of whether money matters should be changed to "money matters for?"[7] Nominal magnitudes are strongly affected by the quantity of money and therefore money matters very much in this context. However, money does not matter for real magnitudes.[8] However, he softens the statement by saying that for real output the quantity of money is not very important, while for prices it is important. He adamantly refutes that he had ever stated or believed that "only money matters," and calls it "absurd."[9]

Keynes and Monetary Theory

The distinction between real and nominal values is not something that an economist should overlook. The difference between them has been pointed out by classical economists dating back to the early 18th century. According to classical economists, nominal economic variables are explained by the quantity theory, with which Keynes agrees. Under the quantity theory, the labor market is competitive and at full employment level. This condition fixes output at its maximum attainable level under the current level of technology. Thus, output cannot increase any further unless technology, capital, or the labor increases. Under this condition, and the assumption of constant velocity, an increase in the supply of money, which increases consumers' purchasing power, causes consumers to bid up prices. Investment cannot increase because the economy is at its full employment capacity. Figure 5.1 depicts the situation. Note that in the northeast quadrant, aggregate supply (AS) is vertical, representing the full employment output level. The southwest quadrant presents a perfectly competitive labor market at equilibrium. The southeast quadrant presents the production function, which is a function of technology and resources. The equilibrium level of labor supply and demand determines AS via the production function. An increase in the supply of money leads to an increase in aggregate demand (AD), which is indicated by a shift to the right. Since AS is perfectly inelastic the price level increases from P_0 to P_1. The result is a reduction in real wages from W_0/P_0 to W_0/P_1, presented in the northwest quadrant. Consequently, an excess demand is created for labor, forcing nominal wages to increase to W_1, where the real wages are the same as before:

$$\frac{W_1}{P_1} = \frac{W_0}{P_0}$$

Missing from the graph and analysis is the Fisher Effect, which represents the increase in the nominal interest rate, and provides another explanation for the lack of increase in investment.[10] Under this analysis the real interest rate after a monetary expansion remains equal to the pre-expansion real interest rate. An implication of this conclusion is that the best thing for the economy is to leave it alone to correct itself when exogenous shocks, such as a discovery of new and less expensive gold, temporarily disturb the long run equilibrium. Keynes objects to this *Laissez-faire* approach and

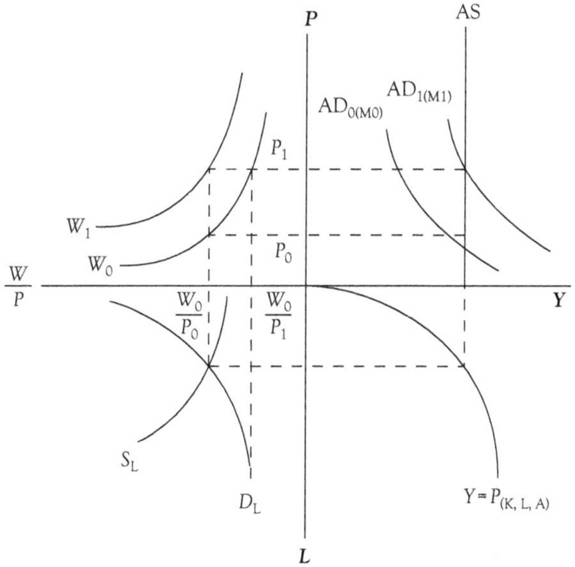

Figure 5.1 Prices under classical economics

advocates the discretionary involvement of government in the economy. It is important to realize that Keynes agrees with the concept that money "does not matter" only when the economy is in full employment. During recessionary periods Keynes does not object to expansionary monetary policy, except in the limited case of the existence of liquidity trap. At least for advocates of *Laissez-faire*, the notion of government intervention, especially through fiscal policy, is of great concern. Among the different fiscal policy instruments, increasing government expenditures through deficit financing used to be less objectionable than paying for it through increased taxes. Consequently, deficit financing has become a habit of most governments. Another possible explanation for deficit financing is that it is more effective than the balanced budget expansionary policy as explained in Chapter 3. In the early decades of the 21st century, the United States is experiencing an objection to deficit financing because of the massive amount of national debt, although the relative amount of budget deficits is not that much higher than previous decades. Figure 5.2 depicts the national debt as the percentage of GDP for the United States.

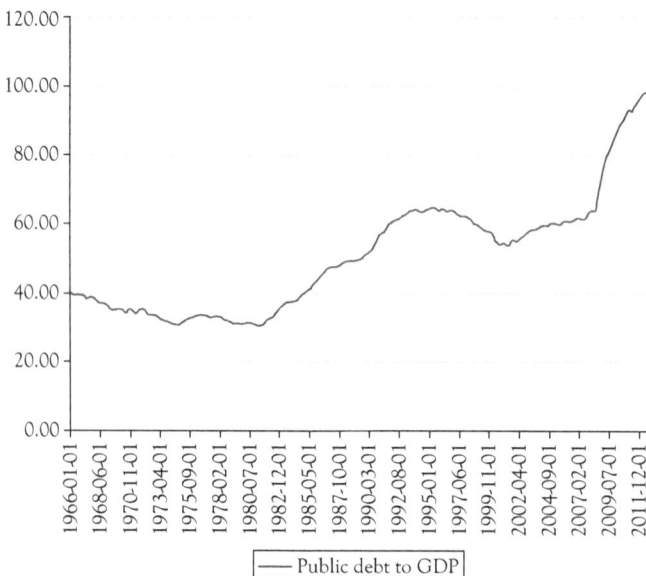

Figure 5.2 National debt as percentage of GDP in United States 1966–2007

Source: Federal Reserve Bank of St. Louis.

Keynes' motive for writing the *General Theory* was to explain business cycles and, more importantly, to eliminate, or at least reduce, their impact. Ever since the Great Depression Keynes was trying to find a way to reduce the high levels of unemployment. In Chapter 1, we explained that marginal capital efficiency, which is calculated based on the present value of the internal rate of return, must be equal to the market interest rate in order for the firms to invest. However, a central argument of Keynes is the lack of responsiveness of investment to shifts in the interest rate due to uncertainty and risk, which are heightened during and shortly after a recession. During such times pessimism about the future and lack of demand for goods hinder investment. It does not make sense for a business to have idle capacity and to plan on increasing its investment. He emphasized the volatility of expectations, the psychology of the public, and increased uncertainty about the future, and concluded that the only possible way for reducing unemployment is through increased government expenditures. Government expenditures increases income and demand, reduces excess capacity, and improves optimism about the future. Uncertainty about the future, especially the future of interest rates and the return on investments, induces people to hold noninterest-bearing cash instead of interest-bearing assets, or reduces investment, regardless of the interest rate.

The Hydraulic Interpretation of Keynes

The IS–LM presentation of Keynesian view introduced by Hicks[11] became the main analytical presentation on the subject. Further contributions by Modigliani,[12] Klein,[13] Samuelson,[14] and Hansen[15] strengthened the subject to the point that this orthodox interpretation dominated the neoclassical school of economics during the 1950s and 1960s. This view is known as the **hydraulic** interpretation. Modigliani[16] shifted the emphasis from volatile expectations to price and wage stickiness, which became widely accepted as the reason for the lack of downward adjustment of wages and prices during economic downturns. Tobin[17] added microeconomic explanations to Keynesian theory. However, the lack of a theoretical explanation for price and wage rigidity is a shortcoming of this group.

The Fundamentalist Interpretation of Keynes

The Keynesian fundamentalists emphasize the role of expectations in forming the behavior of the public, especially during recessionary periods. Prominent members of this view, such as Robinson[18] and Shackle,[19] argue that volatility of expectations is a prominent component of Keynes' theory, especially since he reiterated the issue in his 1937 work.

The Modified General Equilibrium Approach

One way of representing Keynesian economics is to describe it as the economics of disequilibrium since it is focused on the issue of (persistent) unemployment that occurs during recessionary periods, which exemplifies disequilibrium.[20] Patinkin[21] demonstrates that it is possible in a perfectly competitive economy to have unemployment even when prices and wages are flexible. This contribution points out the issue of the time it takes for an economy to adjust itself and return to full employment equilibrium. Leijonhufvud[22] extended this idea to a Walrasian model where markets alone cannot solve the coordination problem. Once it is accepted that prices do not adjust instantaneously in the real economy, there is no reason for an economy not to be able to have adjustment problems, since the price signals are no longer accurate. Leijonhufvud successfully demonstrates that the assumption of instantaneous wage and price adjustment in Walrasian general equilibrium models cannot coexist with incomplete information. Leijonhufvud also points out that according to Keynes' model, the initial reaction to shocks to the economy is adjustments in quantity, not prices. Prices adjust only gradually, and much more slowly than quantities.

CHAPTER 6

Friedman and Modern Quantity Theory

Keynes' *General Theory*[1] introduced new ways of analyzing economics and providing explanations for business cycles. An important contribution is that it demonstrates the possibility that unemployment cannot be resolved automatically. In short, it shows that a market economy need not necessarily succeed in creating and maintaining full employment equilibrium in all markets, at all times. For example, the IS-LM analysis of Chapter 3 reveals the possibility of equilibrium in the goods and money market without equilibrium in the labor market.

After 1936, it seemed that the Walrasian instantaneous auctioneer was dead, and Smith's invisible hand crippled. The idea of discretionary fiscal and monetary policy dominated the attitudes of both economists and policy makers. Even though advocates of fiscal policy agreed that monetary policy had a place in discretionary policy, it was given a supporting role at best and fiscal policy was the main remedy for economic ills. The advocates of discretionary policy claimed that it was possible to eliminate business cycles completely through active government intervention and "fine tuning." For them, displaying the effectiveness of this approach was only a matter of having better analytical tools at their disposal, and more practice. The idea of fine tuning is therefore based on the premise of making smaller and smaller errors in applying fiscal policy and, if necessary, to complement it with monetary policy. The idea of eliminating business cycles implies that it is also possible to have perpetual economic growth without unemployment and recession. In addition, it was thought that through sensible use of monetary policy alongside a discretionary fiscal policy, it is possible to avoid inflation. However, the economic realities of the late 1960s and early 1970s do not support these claims.

Highlights of Classical Quantity Theory

Money is demanded to meet transaction needs, that is, for spending. The demand for money is proportionate to the price level and real income. Output is independent from money and is a function of technology and natural resources; thus, the conclusion that "money does not matter." Its velocity is a function of social, cultural, political, and economic institutions and is either constant or changes very slowly. An increase in the supply of money can only have one effect, an increase in prices. Equation 1.1, the equation of exchange, clearly demonstrates the proportionality of prices and the supply of money, under the above assumptions. However, this equation does not reveal how or why the demand for money is proportionate to income. According to this theory, the level of output is determined exogenously and cannot be influenced by any of the internal forces of the economy. Combining this notion with Smith's invisible hand and Walras's instantaneous auctioneer, the economy is always in equilibrium, except for short adjustment periods after there are external shocks to the system, an idea that was shattered by the Great Depression. In this analysis the supply and demand for (transaction) money determines the price level. Note that classical economists are not saying that the money market determines the price of money, which is the interest rate. Possibly the greatest shortcoming of the classical quantity theory is that its assumptions are not true. There are numerous theoretical challenges to this theory and empirical evidence does not support many of its assumptions.

Pigou's Wealth Formulation

Classical quantity theory, as formulated by Fisher, focuses on demand for money for transactions, which is a **flow** of expenditures. Pigou,[2] on the other hand, focuses on the **stock** of assets. Thus, the question becomes what portion of assets is held in the form of money, rather than what amount of money is demanded for expenditure or consumption. Since Pigou's focus is on holding money rather than spending it, this makes the velocity of money irrelevant and excludes aggregate output from the analysis. The demand equation of Pigou,[3] which is also known as the Cambridge cash balance equation is:

$$M = k\pi R \qquad (6.1)$$

where, M is demand for money, k is the fraction of assets held as money, π is price of assets, and R is real assets. The assets are a function of the supply of money; therefore, k is also a function of supply of money. Note that π is equal to the inverse of P from the equation of exchange. Although there is no explicit reference to velocity in the Cambridge model, the inverse of k is actually the same as the velocity of money in quantity theory. Pigou's contribution is that he applies the microeconomic concept of marginal utility to explain the amount of assets held as money. The proportion of money to other assets is equal to the ratio of their respective marginal utility.

Definition

Marginal utility is the utility derived from the last unit of consuming a good or service.

The conclusion that goods and services are consumed in proportion to their marginal utility is based on the axiom of a diminishing marginal utility of consumption. The idea of a diminishing marginal utility in holding money is a hotly debated issue. Pigou[4] is concerned with holding assets in money and the utility of doing so. He does not state that as more money is obtained its marginal utility diminishes. The notion of a diminishing marginal utility of money is easily refuted by noting that money is a value holder for other goods and services, and, since the human "want" is insatiable, the demand for money is also insatiable. Part of the problem is due to linking the supply of money to the concept of the diminishing marginal utility of holding money. The argument is that when money has diminishing utility an increase in the supply of money should cause a decline in the marginal utility of holding it. However, holding money is a demand issue and cannot be affected by supply factors. The notion that the demand for money can be affected by its supply is similar to the claim that an increase in the output of a good such as corn should reduce the marginal utility of consuming corn. When the corn supply increases, other things equal, its price decreases. With a downward sloping demand curve, a price decrease causes an increase in demand for the good, not a decrease. In microeconomics, goods are consumed until a dollar's worth of each good produces the same marginal utility.

$$\frac{MU_X}{P_X} = \frac{MU_Y}{P_Y} \qquad (6.2)$$

When the price of good x declines it is necessary to increase its consumption to reestablish equality, since under diminishing marginal utility theory as more of a good is consumed its marginal utility declines. This conclusion is supported by reality; as the price of a good declines, other things equal, its consumption increases, provided it is not an inferior good.

Definition

An **inferior good** has negative income elasticity. The demand for an inferior good declines when income increases.

Definition

Income elasticity is a measure of responsiveness of demand for a good to changes in income. It is equal to the ratio of percentage change in demand to a percentage change in income.

Pigou also refers to the utility of money for transaction purposes. He argues that some transactions can be made easily without the need for money and that the utility of money will be nil in such contexts. Some other transactions would be difficult to conduct without money, where the utility of money will be relatively high. Pigou compares the two utilities of using resources to produce goods or to holding these resources in the form of money and suggests they must provide the same utility, that is, have the same marginal utility per dollar's worth.

Under Pigou's demand for money model an increase in the supply of money does not necessarily change prices proportionately or in the same direction. This does not mean that Pigou denies a direct relationship between the supply of money and prices, just that it is not necessarily proportionate or automatic. Pigou[5] states, "I am not in any sense an 'opponent' of the 'quantity theory' or a hostile critic of Professor Fisher's lucid analysis."

Friedman's Modern Quantity Theory of Money

From 1936 to the late 1950s, Keynesian economic theory dominated macroeconomics and fiscal policy was perceived as both the solution to economic disequilibrium and the path to economic growth. Then Friedman[6] revitalized the quantity theory. According to Friedman, the demand for money is proportionate to price level, which implies that the demand for money has a unitary elasticity with respect to the price level. With regard to income, he claims that the income elasticity of demand for money exceeds unity, that is, money is a luxury good. Like Pigou he also subscribed to the notion of money being a type of asset, held for the services it provides.

Friedman also accepts, with some modification, Keynes' argument that demand for money is a function of interest rate. He accepts the application of the opportunity cost concept to the demand for money, which is the interest that would be earned if the money were to be loaned, instead of used for consumption or invested. He also accounts for price increases that devalue money. The relevant price measures are both the price level and rate of increase in prices, or the inflation rate. An increase in the opportunity cost of holding money or the inflation rate reduces the demand for money.

In empirical work Friedman uses permanent income instead of GDP as the measure of income. Friedman says that transitory income does not affect the demand for money while permanent income does. Permanent income represents the expected value of income based on one's history of income and other factors that affect it, such as the level of education, assets, location, gender, and race, to name few. Planned consumption is determined by permanent income. Transitory income and, hence, transitory consumption are not of interest due to random nature of their occurrences. Transitory income is the difference between the expected value of income, or permanent income, and realized income, much like the error term in a regression analysis and statistics.[7] Therefore, Friedman replaces the disposable income of Keynesian models with wealth, which depends on permanent income.

In an attempt to estimate the demand for money and the applicability of his theory Friedman[8] uses the M_2 definition of money and assumes it is not related to income or prices. Therefore, while income and prices cause changes to the supply of money they are not affected by it. The choice of M_2, a broader definition of money than M_1, is believed to contribute to his conclusion that money is a luxury good and that the interest rate does not play an important role in the demand for money. Studies that use the M_1 definition of money conclude that money is a normal good instead of a luxury. It is prudent to keep in mind that the definitions of M_1 and M_2 have changed over time.[9] If the choice of the variable is inappropriate the other results would be biased due to misspecification error. The interest rate means two different things depending on which definition of money is adopted. First, since time deposits pay interest they earn money. Second, demand deposits and currency do not pay interest so the interest rate applicable to M_1 represents its opportunity cost. Therefore, the interest rate cannot be used in models using M_1 in the same context as using the interest rate in models using M_2. The signs for the coefficients of the two "interest rates" are different. The one for time deposit is positive while that of currency and demand deposit are negative. As a result of an increase in the interest rate, demand for time deposits increases while that of currency and demand deposits decreases. Since M_2 contains all three components of money, the opposing signs partially cancel each other out and produce a smaller coefficient than would have existed if the model included only the time deposits.

The modern quantity theory accomplishes several things. First, it reinstates legitimacy to the quantity theory and the role of money. Second, it overcomes the shortcomings of the classical quantity theory by not assuming constant velocity. Third, it incorporates the interest rate into the model, a major shortcoming of the original theory. Fourth, it makes income a function of the supply of money. Interestingly, income is not made completely endogenous by claiming that it does not have any impact on the supply of money. Fifth, it provides a reasonable alternative for fiscal policy. In light of this, one would think that Friedman would advocate replacement of fiscal policy with monetary policy. However, he strongly argued against discretionary stabilization policy, fiscal, or monetary. Instead, he supported the use of policy rules as preference to discretionary policy.

The Process of Market Adjustment

Friedman[10] begins with the assumption that the money market is originally at equilibrium. Let the money supply increase and with it the level of reserves in commercial banks, which can be loaned for investment. As a result, aggregate demand increases and in turn, deposit levels increase as income increases. This process continues until equilibrium is established in the money market. The increased supply of money increases the demand for interest-bearing assets, forcing their prices to increase. In the process, the demand for goods and services increase as well. The result is disequilibrium in the goods market. Contrary to the classical quantity theory, under this scenario both prices and output increase. The process continues until equilibrium is restored in the goods market as well.

By far, the greatest concern with this theory and the process of market adjustment described earlier is the claim that an increase in supply of money causes an increase in real output; hence, an increase in real income. This assumption departs from the notion that money does not matter. Another point that is questioned seriously is the effect of a decline in the interest rate on not only monetary assets, but also real goods, including consumer goods.

CHAPTER 7

Discretionary Policies

Friedman's restatement of the quantity theory in 1956 ended practically 20 years of dominance of the use of discretionary policy through fiscal policy. He addressed the three main problems with the classical quantity theory that allowed fiscal policy to become a viable alternative. The problems were due to unrealistic assumptions that were contrary to evidence, such as the constancy of velocity, disjoint between income and money, and exogeneity of the supply of money. It is possible that changes in supply of money are offset by changes in velocity, that real income might be affected by monetary factors, and that an endogenous money supply makes sense because the FED does not operate in a vacuum. Friedman[1] defines the real demand for money as a function of the nominal rate of return on bonds and equities, the rate of inflation, a wealth factor that is the ratio of human to non-human wealth, real income, and tastes and preferences. This formulation of the quantity theory does not require the constancy of velocity. To Patinkin,[2] Friedman's model is a different version of Keynes' demand for money. At least with regard to his inclusion of the interest rate, Friedman's demand for money is closer to Keynes' demand for speculative money than it is to the classical quantity theory, which does not incorporate the interest rate. However, the dependence of Friedman's model on income is closer to the classical quantity theory than to Keynesian demand for money.

The greatest accomplishment of Friedman is in reviving the quantity theory. Furthermore, Friedman[3] seems to provide a compelling evidence to support his theory of demand for money. In spite of the fact that Friedman makes a case for the effectiveness of monetary policy, he does not support discretionary policy. Part of his opposition is philosophical and part of it is based on economics. Friedman is a great advocate of *laissez-faire*.[4] In monetary theory and policy, however, his advocacy of *laissez-faire* is also based on pragmatic issues. Friedman argues that inside and outside lags have large means and variances.[5] In other words, the length of inside and outside lags are too long for discretionary policies to be effective, which for him includes both fiscal and monetary policies. Of course, he has greater problems with the former as compared to the latter. He is also concerned with changes in the durations of inside and outside lags, that is, the large variances of inside and outside lags, which make their fluctuations less predictable and less reliable. He is also concerned with the difficulty in forecasting the exact position of the economy on a business cycle, the ability to forecast in a timely fashion, and to determine how much discretionary intervention, either fiscal or monetary, is necessary. In Friedman's view, these problems are not related to the inside and outside lags, nevertheless further reduce the effectiveness of the discretionary policies.

Problems with Discretionary Policies

It is essential to be able to determine the exact location of the economy on a business cycle in order to use discretionary policy effectively. Simple magnitudes of economic indicators are not sufficient to make appropriate policy decisions. Figure 7.1 depicts a typical business cycle. The X-axis represents time and the Y-axis represents an economic indicator of interest, customarily GDP. Other reasonable variables include unemployment, the interest rate, and so on. For sake of simplicity, let us use GDP as the economic indicator for policy intervention considerations. At point A the economy is expanding and there is no inflation; thus, there is no reason for discretionary policy, either fiscal or monetary. Had point A been closer to the peak it would have been reasonable to apply contractionary policies to slow the economy down in order to avoid inflation. The discussion here is oversimplified, however. It is important to consider all economic indicators before deciding to employ discretionary policy. For example, if at point A, while the economy is expanding, there is no evidence of inflation, the best policy would be to leave the economy alone, which is the recommendation from laissez-faire advocates, regardless of economic conditions.

At point B, although the GDP is higher than at point A, the economy is contracting and the recommended discretionary policy would be expansionary policies. However, it is unlikely that policymakers or economists would agree to do so. The economist would be reluctant to pursue expansionary policies because the economy is above its long run trend.

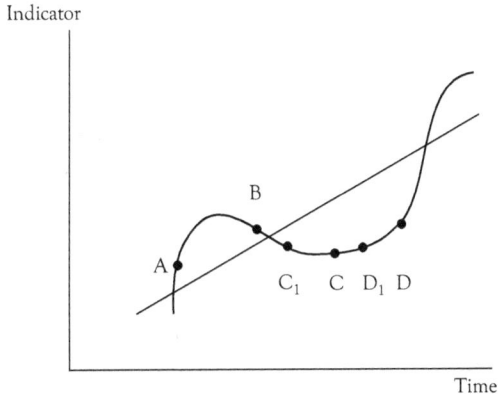

Figure 7.1 Positions on business cycle and discretionary policy

The long run trend is an estimate of the full employment level of output of a country based on its resources, technology, and institutions. Policy makers would be reluctant to accept expansionary policies due to their costs when there is no apparent or pressing problem, such as inflation or substantial unemployment. Point C, however, is different because it is below the trend line and hence the economy could benefit from expansionary policy. It is noteworthy that point C is higher than point A and represents larger GDP. Therefore, it is not the magnitude of the GDP that matters but rather the relative position on the business cycle, which is the important signal. The location on the business cycle for indicators that are based on percentages, such as the unemployment or inflation rate, is also important. Having 6% unemployment on the falling portion of the unemployment cycle requires different action than having 6% unemployment on the rising segment of the cycle. It is important to be aware that unemployment cycles are (somewhat) mirror images of output cycles. Politicians would be reluctant to choose an expansionary policy at point B for the following reasons. It is likely that during the peak just prior to point B the economy suffered from inflation, which is one of the reasons for the turn in the economy from expanding to contracting. Economic expansions continue until a shortage of a resource halts the increase in output and causes prices of that resource to augment until all prices are increasing, which is called inflation. Although at point B the economy begins to contract, it is still in relatively good condition. The level of output is above the long run level and inflation is declining, while unemployment has not yet become a problem. Politically, it is difficult to implement an expansionary policy at this point due to the fear of return of inflation. At points near the peak, such as point B, tax revenues are high, and since governments seldom have the willpower not to spend what is collected, chances are that expenditures are also high. It is difficult in light of the previous discussion to expand expenditures. Finally, tax revenues are lower at point B compared to the peak. This makes it harder for legislators to increase expenditures while revenues are declining and there is no noticeable unemployment.

Troughs like point D on Figure 7.1 are the most likely points for politicians to approve expansionary policies. Most likely, politicians begin the process of considering an action to remedy the economic downturn somewhere prior to point D, and definitely by the time the economy is in the neighborhood of point D, as the pressure to do something is the greatest in such cases. The length of the inside lag is a serious problem here. Suppose the legislator begins the process of approving an expansionary policy at point D_1, but does not succeed in approving it until point D or beyond. By this time the economy has already rebounded and the expansionary policy would hasten the pace of expansion, which may or may not be good for the economy and most likely result in uncontrollable inflation. When the economy is expanding at the rate that it can mobilize its resources, an expansionary intervention could cause bottlenecks in some sectors of the economy. Expanding too rapidly could result in overproduction in some areas that cannot be absorbed by the economy and cause an increase in inventories, which could be interpreted as the return of recession, sometimes referred to as "double-dip" recession.

Pinpointing the Action Time

Anytime the economy is on a downturn and crosses its long run trend line, such as point C_1, it is reasonable to consider an expansionary policy. At first, the economic signals are weak and there is no sense of urgency. However, theoretically, that is the point the action should be considered, if not actually initiated. The exact point depends on the inside lag, which is a political issue influenced by the relative power of the residing president and the party membership of the legislators in the two chambers of Congress in the United States. Friedman and Schwartz,[6] among others, point out that the length of the inside lag is long and that fluctuations of this length make it difficult to obtain a useful estimate for each specific economic downturn. Therefore, it is necessary to accurately estimate the size of GDP, the location of the economy in the business cycle, the length of time the economy would take to reach the trough from that point, and the inside lag before being able to proceed with a discretionary policy.

It is also necessary to identify the appropriate policy instrument. Unfortunately, there is normative bias among economists on whether fiscal or monetary policy is more effective. The normative bias may be even greater among politicians as each particular policy affects their constituents; hence, it affects their political future in different ways and to varying extents. These factors also contribute to the length of the inside lag.

After a choice between monetary and fiscal policy is made it is necessary to identify the most effective tool for the situation on hand. This selection of a tool should be the least controversial and problematic among all the issues pertaining to these two policies. Once a tool is selected it is necessary to determine the magnitude of the remedy and to estimate how long it would be before signs of improvement should emerge; this is the outside lag, which Friedman and Schwartz[7] estimated to be long with a large variance as well. The larger the magnitude of the suggested solution the more difficult it would be to implement it.

Friedman's View on Discretionary Policy

Friedman argues that monetary tools are very potent and effective in affecting economic variables, most notably, the ones in his demand for money model discussed in Chapter 6. Nevertheless, because of the issues enumerated in the previous section he suggests that the money supply should not be used as a policy instrument. Imagine a pendulum on the swing that is pushed toward the resting point when it is off the target. The push will augment the inertia already stored in the pendulum as a result of its swing away from equilibrium. The result of the push toward equilibrium or the resting point augments the stored energy and makes it swing more than it would have otherwise. Therefore, Friedman advocates a rule that requires a constant rate of growth for the supply of money equal to the estimated long run trend of economic growth adjusted for the rate of growth of population.

There are several advantages for having a well-publicized rule for a stable growth rate of the money supply. Notice that in the previous sentence we chose the word "rule" instead of "policy." This is a deliberate choice since once discretion is taken away the resulting act is based on a rule. In fact, the discussion of rules versus discretion is an important ongoing issue.[8] Friedman suggests legislation that promotes a steady and constant increase in the supply of money, preferably daily, for a cumulative total of about 3–5% growth per year.[9] The actual magnitude is not important and the suggested value solely reflects the economic reality of the time. The important thing is that this increase should be steady, constant, and well publicized. His recommendation is based in part on the permanent income hypothesis, according to which customary consumption is a function of permanent income, not transitory income, and in part on the belief that the supply of money directly affects income. Surprise changes in the supply of money are perceived and transitory.

Friedman is also against locking the money supply growth rate at a fixed rate regardless of economic conditions. He believes that the long run economic growth rate and population growth rate must be used to estimate the necessary rate of growth of money, which would have small changes as a result. In an analogy to a ship he points out that it would not make sense to set the helm for the desired course and then lock it in position. Instead, a compass should be used for guidance and the helm for dealing with the ongoing conditions of the sea. In his later writings Friedman allowed for greater margin on the rule.

The other contributing factor to the discretionary policy was the mounting evidence against the Phillips[10] Curve.

Definition

Phillips Curve refers to the empirical evidence of tradeoff between inflation and unemployment.

Rushing to conclusion, a causal relationship between the rate of unemployment and inflation was established, which was soon translated into a fiscal policy instrument.[11] Samuelson and Solow[12] were instrumental in recommending the use of Phillips Curve as a policy instrument. Accordingly, when unemployment is high the government would intervene and reduce it, with the price of this policy being increased inflation. On the contrary, when inflation becomes too high it could be lowered at the cost of increased unemployment. The work by Friedman[13] casts major doubt on the validity of the hypothesis. The Phillips Curve was the result of unexpected inflation, but by the mid-1970s the unexpectedness was gone; thus, the relationship also vanished. Friedman[14] and Phelps[15] disprove the effectiveness of the Phillips Curve. Subsequent works on the rational expectations hypothesis effectively invalidated the Phillips Curve.[16]

Friedman[17] modifies his stance on the fixed rate of money growth to that of a steady rate. He keeps the predictability and low magnitude requirements. He also favors a simple rule because it is easier to understand and would gain more public support than a more sophisticated rule. These recommendations are substantially different than his earlier position in 1948, which advocates the government should exercise a fiscal policy compatible with full employment. This means that the government should maintain a surplus, that is, collect more taxes than it spends during expansionary periods, and to allow deficits during recessionary periods, that is, collect less tax than it spends. He opposes deficit financing through changes in the money supply rather than through bonds. Since automatic stabilizers do not have inside lags he advocates full control of the supply of money by requiring 100% reserve for commercial banks, which means to strip banks from creating any money. Sometimes the 100% reserve requirement is proposed for checking accounts only. Under 100% reserve system, commercial banks must find other sources of income, such as charging fees for transactions and even charging fees on deposits, in order to cover their costs and earn a reasonable return on their investment. A 100% reserve requirement effectively converts the credit money system to a commodity money system. However, Friedman's later stance[18] tones down the need for automatic stabilizers, yet insists that the fixed exchange rate in existence under the Bretton Woods agreement be eliminated. The French were also advocating this at the time, with objections from the United States. However, after 1968, there is no trace of the recommendation of a 100% reserve requirement in Friedman's writings.

SECTION III

Schools of Thought in Monetary Theory

CHAPTER 8

Austrian School

Over the years several schools of thought have developed, each of which encompasses its own philosophy and interpretation of reality. The doctrines and assumptions of these schools reflect their underlying philosophies. Consequently, their anticipated and expected outcomes in response to different economic conditions and events are different. The recommended policy responses are also different. This chapter provides a brief summary of the major highlights of some of the more prominent theories.

Austrian School and Business Cycle Theory

Menger[1] advanced the concept of marginality, which changed microeconomic analysis. Analysis of value based on the last unit of consumption provided an explanation for the water and diamond paradox. Classical economics were unable to explain why water, an essential substance for life, was very cheap, while diamonds, which at the time had only ornamental use, were very expensive.

The importance of microeconomic theory in macroeconomics dates back to Bohm-Bawerk.[2] Mises[3] uses marginal utility to determine the value of money. Hayek[4] combines Menger's capital theory and the theory of money and credit by Mises to form the business cycle theory of the Austrian school. With regard to production, orthodox macroeconomics focuses on factor markets, similar to trade studies, and product markets, similar to microeconomics. This static view of the production process is replaced by a dynamic process in the Austrian school, which also considers intermediate goods. These types of goods are outputs of earlier processes, yet they are inputs for later processes. Consumer goods are called first order, producer goods are called second order, and the ranking continues for all types of intermediate goods until the raw materials level is reached, which contains no other products.

The foundation of the Austrian school is based on the use of capital and the fact that each stage of production yields an output that is used by the next stage; a process that continues until a final good is produced for consumption. Each stage adds value to the output of the previous stage. Intermediate goods might be produced and used within one firm or purchased from other firms without affecting the discussion at hand. The forces that set the production process in motion originate from the value of consumer goods. Menger's Law states that the anticipated value of the final product causes a derived demand for the intermediate products down the production chain.

Definition

Derived demand is a demand for a product when its use does not provide direct utility. The product is demanded because it is used in the production of other goods or services, which provide direct utility.

Another essential component of this school of thought is the central role of an entrepreneur. Entrepreneurs must forecast the future value of a final product, assess the market value of each intermediate good, and apply the discount value to all temporal activities in order to be able to determine whether the production would be worthwhile and the return on investment would be no less than the market interest rate. Furthermore, in the temporal process of production, marginal changes can and do occur at any stage. The cumulative effects of these marginal changes, especially when they are in the same direction, cause business cycles.

Economic Growth

Economies grow positively or negatively over time. When investment exceeds depreciation, that is, net investment is positive, the growth rate is positive. When gross investment is just enough to replace depreciation the economy would be stationary, which neoclassical economists call the steady state. This argument does not apply when technology improves. Assume no change in technology or resources; instead, assume an intertemporal preference changes in favor of the future. This change in intertemporal preferences requires a change from producing consumer goods for present consumption to investment goods that will be used to produce goods for future consumption. Without a reduction in current consumption it is not possible to increase future output; hence, consumption. The duration of sacrifice depends on the inter-temporal value of future consumption. The greater the value of future consumption the greater the need for a reduction in current consumption and the longer the length of time before consumption will be equal to the original consumption level.

The opposite preference can have a devastating effect on a country. When current consumption becomes more valuable than future consumption it is necessary to divert expenditures from investment, that is, production of goods for production purposes, to consumer goods. This reduces the production capacity of the economy and can eventually result in destruction of the economy, if continued. Since inter-temporal consumption choice is a consumer choice issue, the market economy is capable of allocating resources to reflect people's preferences and maximize their utilities. One problem with this simplified notion of growth is its neglect of what happens when investment increases just enough so that total gross investment only replaces depreciated capital. Without technological advancements this outcome is inevitable.

In this analysis there is no role for the government to play, except perhaps for creating appropriate institutions that allow the economy to accommodate consumer choices and preferences. Implicit in this, but never acknowledged, is that consumer's self-interest and preference for current over future consumption could potentially destroy the production capacity of the economy.

The Role of Savings

The inter-temporal allocation of resources highlighted in the previous paragraph may not materialize due to internal forces of the economy. The existence of a mechanism that can translate consumer choices inter-temporally is essential. The mechanism must generate sufficient savings to make the investments necessary to materialize the desired level of future consumption. A simplistic response is that market forces will efficiently allocate resources between investment and consumption according to their prices. An increase in the preference for one will increase its price relative to the other. While these issues and concerns are handled well in microeconomics, at the macro level other concerns have to be contemplated.

According to Keynes there is no mechanism that links decisions for present consumption with decisions to plan for making future consumption. Unlike monetarists, Keynes separates output for consumption from output for production, which is the same as investment. Austrian models divide output into intermediate products in the production chain. Therefore, in the latter, the production of capital goods is ranked before the production of final consumer goods. The problem is that different decision makers represent different groups of consumers and producers, and the preferences of the former must be relayed, somehow, to the latter. Monetarists, however, claim that the supply of money is the relevant factor for all macroeconomic issues. Consequently, they completely ignore issues that pertain to intermediate goods, both in the short and long run. At the macro level only the aggregates matter.

Signaling Consumers' Wishes to Producers

The classical economists argue that consumers signal their preferences by changing their demand, which in turn affects prices. Producers maximize their profits by producing goods in high demand, as signaled by an increase in their prices, and cutback on the production of goods whose prices are declining. This mechanism does not work for inter-temporal preferences because future goods are not yet produced and cannot be traded, thus their prices cannot be determined in the market place. Therefore, the signal must come from another source.

One way of signaling preferences for future consumption is to increase savings. At the consumer level this implies a desire to consume less at the present and to use that savings to consume more in the future. So the market receives two signals: a reduction in current consumption and an increase in savings. An overall decrease in current consumption dampens aggregate (current) demand, which signals producers to reduce production. Customarily, this is accomplished by a reduction in employment and a decision not to replace depreciated capital, that is, a reduction in investment. This latter decision is contrary to the desire of consumers for increased future consumption. In the Austrian model the demand for intermediate goods, which are inputs for the production of the next stage, show a reduction, similar to a ripple effect. The increase in savings reduces the interest rate; thus reducing the cost of holding inventory.

The magnitude of the impact varies by industry and for different products. Intermediate goods further down the chain and away from the consumption goods, and those that are costly and large in size, would benefit most from a reduction in the interest rate. The ability to foresee the potential demand for future goods is an essential determinant of the decision to engage in the production of higher-order intermediate goods, which constitutes the early stages of production toward final consumer goods. Keynes interpreted increased saving as a reduction in aggregate demand; therefore, savings was contractionary. In the Austrian model the question is what is the purpose of increase in savings? An increase in savings for the purpose of increasing consumption in the future is a signal to increase production, not to reduce it. According to the Austrian school, an entrepreneur is someone who can correctly recognize the signal to change production in the correct direction.

The amount of income not utilized for current consumption is closely related to the output that is not intended for consumption. The latter is called investment while the former is called savings. The income not intended for current consumption constitutes the source of loanable funds. The owner of these funds could be consumers or producers who have set aside part of their incomes or revenues for the purpose of investment. Under Keynesian economics, savings is always equal to investment, while under the loanable funds theory the two are equal only at the equilibrium level of interest rate. In Keynesian terminology, savings is actually what is not consumed, yet is also not used for investment. It is the money that is taken out of circulation; thus, it is contractionary. Changes in this type of savings reflect changes in liquidity preferences in Keynesian theory. Therefore, a major distinction among the Austrian school, Keynesian theory, and modern quantity theory, is that the former believes the interest rate is determined in the loanable funds market while the latter two settle the matter as part of the demand for money, or liquidity preference.

Austrian Macroeconomics

According to the Austrian School the interest rate at the equilibrium level is considered the natural rate. Changes in inter-temporal consumption preferences affect both savings and the natural rate of interest. The natural rate of interest is unknown *a priori* but governs equilibrium in the capital market, hence, the entire economy. Any attempt to set or move the interest rate differently or away from the natural rate will result in disequilibrium in the market. Without government intervention, an increase in savings, or equivalently an increase in the inter-temporal preference for future consumption, the natural rate of interest declines and reduces the cost of investment. This spurs an increase in investment, which is believed to offset the decline in demand due to the initial increase in saving. Thus, the economy stays on its production possibility frontier. Although the economy remains on the same production possibility frontier, the mix of output has changed from consumer goods to mostly intermediate goods at the bottom of the production process.

It is not clear what assurances exist for the equality of output after the change with output before the change, which assures the economy remains on its production possibility frontier. It would seem that the only alternative to remaining on the production possibility frontier is to be inside it, representing a loss of production. However, this argument is not necessarily valid at all times. An economy can produce above its production possibility frontier, at least temporarily, while it is in transition. Working people might work overtime and people not in the labor market might conclude that entering the job market is more lucrative and seek to obtain jobs. Once the transition is complete, the level of output will be somewhere on the production possibility frontier because technology and resources determine the production capacity of the economy. Changes in the natural rate, and the pursing changes in investment, will cause mobility of resources from one stage of production to another in response to market signals. In the Austrian school, producing beyond the production possibility frontier is called mal-investment.

The MPC is fairly stable under the Keynesian model. Consequently, MPS = 1 − MPC is also stable. Therefore, Keynesians do not expect great changes in savings. At a less extreme view, savings is inelastic with respect to the interest rate. An increase in savings can only occur as a result of decrease in the MPC. Such a decline causes the denominator of the multiplier to become larger. Therefore, the multiplier effect becomes smaller, rendering fiscal policy less effective, as well as triggering a contractionary process that can lead to recession. An increase in savings will result in a decline in output, which is the same as moving from a point on the production possibility frontier to somewhere inside the curve, representing a loss of production capacity. This dilemma is also known as the paradox of thrift.[5] In Keynesian models the interest rate will remain the same, regardless of the amount of savings, as long as the supply and demand for money remain unchanged. The discussion assumes other things remain the same, including investment, which is contrary to the core of the Austrian models.

Business Cycle Theory

According to the Austrian model market economies work. This should not be taken as a declaration that disequilibrium does not exist in this model. For example, in a classical model disequilibrium is caused by external forces and is a temporary phenomenon that can exist only during transitions toward equilibrium. The main philosophical distinction between the Austrian school and Keynesianism is that the latter believes the market can and will fail while the former believes the market will correct itself. Austrian economists view reduction in output as a deliberate act to increase production in the future due to increased inter-temporal preference for future consumption. Therefore, a recession is nothing more than a period of increased investment, which may not manifest itself in increased consumer goods because, initially, only the production of the lower-level intermediate goods increases. Thus, Austrian theory accepts the existence of business cycles. This school considers business cycles a necessary part of the market economy for the translation of the utility maximizing preferences of consumers for present and future consumption. In turn, this allows producers to adjust their behavior in pursuit of maximizing their profits. Under this theory any exogenous intervention in the economy will result in disequilibrium. The advocates of the Austrian School do not deny the claim that the government could reduce the interest rate and that it would result in increased output. Nevertheless, their point is that such an exogenous increase is not accompanied by changes in savings or inter-temporal consumption preferences. Thus, it is not sustainable and the market economy will correct the situation by a return to the pre-intervention position.

Under the Austrian theory, during an expansion the production of consumer goods and intermediate goods toward the bottom increases. The former increases to satisfy demand, while the latter increases to satisfy anticipated increased future demand. Eventually, this causes enough distortion in the economy to end the boom and start a bust. Discretionary policies increase the production of consumer goods, while also possibly reducing investment to replace depreciated machinery, which can also include maintenance. The process is hastened by an increase in prices in areas where shortages are not able to sustain the artificially high production levels. In short, it is not supported by an increase in savings, which have not materialized due to the lack of inter-temporal preferences for future consumption.

This analysis is in sharp contrast to the Keynesian aggregate demand-induced expansionary policies. In other words, Keynesian macroeconomics is oblivious to the effect of the interest rate on investment in intermediate goods. The Austrian business cycle focuses on resource allocation to the point of ignoring changes in prices and wages in a business cycle. While Keynesians believe government intervention in the market economy is inevitable due to inherent problems that can lead to unemployment, the Austrian theory deems the market economy is effective in returning itself to equilibrium unless the economic signals are distorted as a result of government intervention.

Even when the economy is growing at a high rate the Austrian school opposes easy money policy to accommodate and facilitate growth. In fact, under this theory, expansionary credit has no impact on growth and can actually cause a real increase in prices that might more than offset growth-induced nominal price decreases. When expansionary monetary policy is accompanied with an increase in output rather than prices, monetarists claim victory for the power of monetary theory. Although price stability during periods of growth might be welcome news to many, the Austrian theory considers it a sign of trouble because the lack of a price increase will signal producers to slowdown production. Once again, government intervention would distort the economy and create problems.

CHAPTER 9

Rational Expectations Hypothesis

Most economic activities and decisions extend into the future, which makes them either uncertain or risky. Expectations about the future are important in economic decisions. Each individual has to forecast what will happen in the future and how future outcomes will affect their current plans and economic activities. This is true even if individuals have no formal training in forecasting and their level of sophistication or ability is low. Different people have different expectations about the future, which is affected in part by their current situations, needs, and plans.

Nowhere is this concept demonstrated better than in a stock market. The old cliché "buy low sell high" is well known, and it is supposed to be the golden rule of trade in the stock market. However, anytime an exchange takes place the seller thinks he or she is selling high, while the buyer believes he or she is buying low, or there would not be any motive to engage in the transaction. This holds true regardless of any differences in individuals' needs at the time of exchange. For example, a retired investor could be cashing his funds to maintain his or her standard of living during his or her golden years while a newly employed investor is planning for his or her children's college or retirement. These examples highlight the need for forecasting. In the first example, if the seller believes the price of his or her stock would be higher tomorrow he or she would, most likely, wait another day. Similarly, the buyer in the second example will not part from his or her money if he or she believes tomorrow's stock price will be lower.

People make transaction decisions based on their expectations about future. Although this is a formidable task, determining how other people come to their forecasts about future is even harder. Of course, forecasting the future for oneself, or on behalf of others, would be easy if accuracy was not required.

Adaptive Expectations

Theories about expectation formation are compelled to make an assumption of rationality. This is because it is not possible to forecast irrational behavior. It is also necessary to assume, as is customary in economics, that people maximize their utility by making the right choices. This does not mean that all forecasts are, or should be, accurate or correct. However, it is necessary to assume that the forecasts are not systematically wrong. Another way of stating the same concept is that people learn from their mistakes and that they are capable of taking corrective measures to reduce the frequency and magnitude of their mistakes. Whether these assumptions are true in real life is not known to researchers. However, these assumptions are vital for formation of a model to forecast the future.

Definition

Adaptive expectations mean that expectations change gradually and incrementally.

One alternative to the rationality assumption is the naïve forecast. In the naïve forecast the value of the next period is believed to be the same as the current value of the phenomenon to be forecasted. An adaptive expectation version of the naïve forecast is to add the magnitude of error of its forecast for the previous period to the current period's value to obtain the next period's forecast. Suppose inflation in period one is 2%. In the naïve forecast, expected inflation for period two is 2%. Now suppose inflation for period two happens to be 2.5% instead. The forecast was off by 0.5%, so the actual inflation for period two is modified by the amount of error, and the forecast for the third period is 2.5 + 0.5 = 3%. Therefore, adaptive expectations are based on historical data and change gradually. In reality, people too, adjust their forecasts gradually. Suppose that, for a while, expected inflation ranges between 0% and 5%. It might take several periods of 5% inflation before people adjust their expectations to anticipate the inflation for the next period to be 5%. Forecasts will be more accurate if one could identify the sources for changes in the phenomenon of interest. For example, the quantity theory posits that an increase in the supply of money causes inflation. Repeated inflations after each increase in supply of money will suggest a causal relationship and people will form their expectations of inflation based on the magnitude of changes in supply of money.

Rational Expectations

Muth[1] hypothesizes that individuals' expectations are the same as the expected outcomes predicted by economic theory. Information gained from mistakes will be used to improve future expectations. It is important to realize that in order for the expected, or average, value to be a certain value it is necessary for some observation to be smaller than the mean while others are higher. In order for the expected inflation to be 5% some forecasts of inflation must be below 5% while others must be above it. The unrealistic case in which everyone's forecast is identical is the only exception. The probability of exactly identical forecasts is low because information is costly and different economic agents have varied economic experiences about a particular phenomenon. Recall that repeated and frequent forecasts improve the accuracy of the forecast. Since information is expensive, the economy does not waste information. Muth asserts two conclusions from studies of expectations:

1. Averages of expectations in an industry are more accurate than naïve models and as accurate as elaborate equation systems, although there are considerable cross-sectional differences of opinion.
2. Reported expectations generally underestimate the extent of changes that actually take place.

Rational expectations hypothesis claims that economic agents' expectations are scattered about the predicted values of economic theory, provided the information set remains constant. This hypothesis asserts that information is scarce, expectations depend on the structure of the economic system, and that public predictions do not affect the economic system by much, if at all. Muth[2] does not require entrepreneurs to utilize statistical equations and methods. Nor does his hypothesis require, or imply, that all predictions are correct or the same.

Following statistical methods, deviations of observed outcomes from expected outcomes are called errors.[3] These errors are assumed to follow a normal distribution function, a common practice in statistics. For simplicity the models are assumed to be linear. The final assumption is the existence of "certainty equivalents." The premise of this hypothesis is that on the average, economic agents will correctly expect the outcome stated by economic theory. This concept is similar to the mathematical concept of expectation. It can be shown that the sum, and hence the average, of deviations from the mean is zero. Thus, average errors are zero. The implication is that forecasts are unbiased.

Mathematical expectations are calculated using appropriate formulas based on the distributional properties of the phenomenon under study. Studies based on the rational expectations hypothesis utilize sophisticated statistical tools and mathematical equations. A major accomplishment of the rational expectations hypothesis is its successful use of statistical thinking and interpretation. An important point to remember is that the individual errors need not be zero; only that their expected value, that is, their average is zero. A zero expected error indicates that on the average economic agents do not make mistakes, and there is no systematic bias in the expectation of future economic outcomes. Rational expectations hypothesis claims that the outcome of repeated experimentations with reality allows economic agents to mimic the mathematical formulas. Theories that are not based on rational expectations implicitly allow systematic errors in expectations. Note that this claim is not as outrageous as it might initially sound, since the science of statistics is based on real life outcomes and the resulting theories reflect typical events in life.

As new data becomes available, expectations are recalculated and new estimates are obtained. The importance of distant information gradually diminishes, and sooner or later, they are removed from the analysis. The greater the event and its impact, the longer it influences future expectations. Major events such as the Great Recession of 2008 will affect the expected value of economic activities for a long time. One of the first applications of the rational expectations hypothesis was to discredit the Phillips Curve.

According to the Phillips Curve,[4] policy makers may choose to reduce either unemployment or inflation. The price of choosing to reduce unemployment or inflation is an increase in the other one. When in the 1970s, evidence to the contrary manifested, it was the rational expectations hypothesis that proved the fallacy of the relationship.[5] When the cost of information increases the ability to form and update expectations decreases. When information is lacking, the error in expectation increases. Thus, the accuracy of expectations decreases as the frequency of shocks and availability of information decreases. These conclusions are the same as those in mathematical expectations. The premise of rational expectations hypothesis, with regard to any outcome in which probability plays a role and discretionary interventions are possible, is that people cannot be fooled forever. This is similar to the cliché that some people can be fooled sometimes, but all people cannot be fooled all the time. The collapse of the Phillips Curve ended the notion that it is possible for fiscal policy to tradeoff unemployment for inflation and vice versa, which is the same as the ability to fool the public for ever.

Rational Expectations hypothesis fails if full information is not available, or it is not worth spending the time and effort to form rational expectations. The more important the consequences of a decision, the more time, effort, and expenses have to be devoted to information to be able to form rational expectations. For example, little time is devoted to determine which store sells the cheapest cabbage, while lots of time will be spent researching neighborhoods, schools, value appreciation, quality of neighborhood, and so forth when purchasing a house. Similarly, businesses are far more careful when deciding on major investments than in dealing with mundane concerns.

A natural outcome of rational expectations is that when economic variables change, or when factors that determine other economic factors are altered, expectations must also be modified. Implicit in this statement is the assumption of availability of information. Thus, the benefits of changing expectations must offset the cost of modification in order for economic agents to change their expectations.

The randomness of errors, that is, deviations of expectations from theoretical values, implies that individual errors are not estimable. The fact that the average of errors is zero indicates that there is no systematic bias in expectations. Similarly, the expectations of economic agents need not to be exactly the same as the theoretical value, but their deviations from expected values will converge to zero.

Efficient Market Hypothesis

The application of rational expectations hypothesis in the financial market is known as the efficient market hypothesis, or the theory of efficient capital markets. Concepts of the efficient market hypothesis and rational expectations hypothesis were developed in two different areas of finance and economics. Muth[6] is the starting point for both hypotheses. The jargons for the two, however, are different.

A profitable endeavor in financial circles is publication of financial advice in the form of books and reports. Under the best scenario, this advice is based on existing information. Thus, it does not provide any advantage to forming overall expectations and is useless. Under a more cynical scenario, they are simply hoaxes and the authors do not utilize all available information. The efficient market hypothesis implies that the probability of earning unusually high, or low, returns on investment is almost zero. Thus, the hot tips from advisors and brokers have no real value in outperforming the expected outcome of the market on the average. These are based on existing information and since they do not add any new information; they are worthless. This is not the same as "insider information," which is only available to people that have unusual access to information, such as members of Congress, employees of companies, or stock brokers. The use of such restricted information for personal gain is prohibited by insider trading law.

The Effect of Expectations

Rational Expectations hypothesis does not indicate, or even imply, that peoples' expectations determine future outcomes. Every time something happens or something changes it also affects expectations. For example, when a major bank has financial problems it affects expectations about that bank, the banking system, government deficits, the growth rate, stock prices, and in short, the entire economy. Any new information is used to form new expectations. In such a case, there are people who over-react while others under-react. The overreaction or under-reaction is with regard to the outcome of the effect as predicted by economic theory, and it is not an arbitrary opinion of one person or the other. These deviations from expected values are random and cancel each other out. When the new event occurs no one has sufficient information to determine its full consequences for economic outcomes. Therefore, people will react based on their formed expectations. Eventually, the average of these expecta-tions will converge to the theoretically correct outcome. Additionally, beliefs that are formed on the basis of ideology, political orientation, reli-gious belief, or other noneconomic perceptions do not affect economic outcomes. Shear speculative beliefs do not affect real economic phenom-ena. For example, the belief that recession will occur will not cause a recession just because people expect it, as this expectation is not based on economic reality.

Dynamic Inconsistency

It is possible that the preferences of a decision maker will change over time. When new preferences are inconsistent with the original prefer-ences, the original course of action can no longer yield an optimal out-come under new circumstances. Since the issue involves time, the subject is dynamic. Dynamic inconsistency is an integral part of game theory, where a dynamically inconsistent game is shown to produce suboptimal outcomes. A policy-maker-established inflation rate might be a preferred choice at the time of making the decision, but not necessarily when the actual future date has arrived. Dynamic inconsistency is one of the rea-sons for the superiority of policy rules over discretion. It can be shown that, in order to reduce the social cost on monetary policy, policy makers must adopt an inflation rate rule. The problem lies not in choosing but in maintaining that rule. Failure to maintain the rule would result in lack of credibility and cause the policy to fail.

Rational Expectations and Policy Implications

The contribution of rational expectations hypothesis is not that it introduces the idea of expectations into economics. As economic phenomena depend on expectations of future outcomes, the contribution is in incorporating mathematical expectations into economic modeling and in making expectations endogenous. The use of mathematical expectations rules out the possibility of systematic bias in the formation of expectations about economic outcomes. A byproduct of incorporating mathematical statistics into the subject is the increasing complexity of the literature. For example, in order to comprehend Muth,[7] it is necessary to have a solid command of both statistics and mathematics.

Rational expectations cannot be formed without full information. Since information is costly it is possible that some expectations have to be formed without full knowledge of all the facts. Such expectations need not, and usually do not, agree with the results predicted by rational expectations hypothesis. Expensive information has similar limiting effects. Random shocks introduced into the economy by the government confuse economic agents and increase the cost of obtaining information. Ironically, frequent government intervention is better than infrequent intervention because the former enables economic agents to learn to predict the outcome of government interventions correctly. However, the lesson is expensive and it is better to have transparency and consistency. These ideas are similar to Friedman's recommendation of setting a constant growth rate for the supply of money as a rule and making it well publicized. Friedman's next recommendation is that the government must adhere to its broadcasted policy. In essence, Friedman advocates a policy rule.

One advantage of a rule is that it is known. During World War II the economy of France witnessed repeated money supply shocks; each of which was followed by a price increase. In time, economic agents learned to expect the outcome and adjusted their conduct accordingly. Consequently, anytime the government broadcasted an increase in the supply of money over the radio, the shopkeeper changed their prices to reflect the pursuing (anticipated) inflation; thus, keeping real prices constant. This behavior was used as evidence that money does not matter because the changes in prices nullified the increase in the supply of money without affecting real economic variables like output. Although this is a correct example supporting the rational expectations hypothesis, and economists of the time were using it as evidence of the role and importance of expectations, they were nonetheless incorporating such expectations into their models exogenously.

Criticism of Rational Expectations Hypothesis

Critics of rational expectations hypothesis point out that information is not always available. It is costly, and average businessmen or entrepreneurs do not have the economic knowledge to know the theoretically expected outcome, let alone average individuals with no formal training. Some critics point out that even professional economists do not agree on the expected outcome of the economy in the future. The presumption and misunderstanding is that critics believe it is essential for economic agents to know the expected outcome of the economy in order for their conduct to reflect the theoretically expected outcome. In fact, the theory assumes no economic training or the ability to forecast the future.

The ability of economic agents to correctly predict theoretic economic outcomes without formal economic education can be explained. First, economic theories reflect how the economy functions and what causes it to change. Therefore, they are explaining the reality, which is the result of the interaction of people in response to changes in economic factors. It is not necessary to know economics to comply with economic realities. In a discussion of the use of assumptions in economics, Friedman[8] "explains" the density of leaves around a tree. Leaves "choose" an appropriate location on a branch to optimize the amount of light necessary for the particular species of tree. Another example from economics might be beneficial. Friedman[9] points out that "expected returns (generally, if misleadingly, called "profits") . . . refer to the difference between actual and "expected" results, between *ex post* and *ex ante* receipts. "Profits" are then a result of uncertainty and, as Alchain [1950]..., following Tintner, points out, cannot be deliberately maximized in advance." The only requirement for the rational expectations hypothesis is that economic agents act as if they know the structure of the actual economy.

CHAPTER 10

Inflation Targeting

Inflation targeting is proposed by Taylor.[1] Inflation targeting is a modified version of Friedman's[2] proposal of a fixed growth rate for money supply. McCallum[3] proposes a 3% growth rate for the supply of money, which is adjusted in response to changes in the growth rate of nominal gross national product (GNP). The foundation of inflation targeting is formed by the rational expectations hypothesis. The hypothesis demonstrates that indiscriminate use of monetary, fiscal policy, or both would teach economic agents to anticipate their consequences and correct their behavior accordingly; thus rendering discretionary policy ineffective over time. The ineffectiveness of monetary policy is a prominent component of the real business cycle theory, as well. Consequently, the best policy is to have a transparent monetary policy that is well publicized and pursued diligently. Under such conditions, monetary policy can become very effective in achieving targeted objectives, such as a particular rate of inflation.

McCallum[4] points out that both the rational expectations hypothesis and empirical evidence are important in the formation of an inflation targeting rule. At least in the United States, the initial impression are that there has been no economic theory for the formation of inflation targeting rule and that the alleged use of one by the Fed has been the result of political pressure.

Taylor[5] adopts an analytic approach to policy evaluation to obtain a policy tool. In this approach a dynamic model is created using alternative approaches from macroeconomic, fiscal, and monetary theories, which are then used to perform a simulation using dynamic stochastic procedures. Taylor[6] calls this approach "new normative macroeconomics." It is normative because the outcome is used to make policy recommendations to achieve specific objectives.

The term "rule" is only partially correct in this context. The rule is modified periodically based on the output gap, which is the difference between the actual real GDP and its expected value. Customarily, the trend line of GDP for a country is used as the expected, or full-employment, GDP. This is different from the simple rule of a constant growth rate of money proposed by Friedman.[7] Inflation targeting and Friedman's constant rule share the view that monetary policy should be stable, publicized, and diligently pursued to allow the public to form reliable expectations about it and its outcome. In this sense, inflation targeting is a form of rational expectations hypothesis, and as such, it indicates that transparent and persistent policies allow appropriate and consistent responses from economic agents. Rational expectations hypothesis demonstrates that under these conditions the expected behaviors of economic agents will coincide with their theoretically predicted outcomes.

The theoretical foundation of inflation targeting incorporates existing macroeconomic and monetary theories as well as the rational expectations hypothesis. The actual inflation targeting, however, does not provide grounds for any theoretical discussion; it is a normative policy recommendation. For example, when an economic downturn becomes severe and there is a possibility of a recession, the recommended policy is to decrease the interest rate. Recall this is exactly what Friedman opposed on the ground that it is not clear when the economy has slowed enough to warrant government interventions. By the time the recession is declared it might already be too late to take expansionary actions. It is also difficult to forecast the severity of the recession. The counterpoint Taylor[8] makes is that "feedback rules in which the money supply responds to changes in unemployment or inflation are also policy rules." This interpretation of a policy rule is different from the constant growth rate of the yesteryears, when the debate between discretion and rule was more acute.

The Taylor Rule is a policy rule that is implemented loosely, and policy makers use their judgment to intervene in the application of the rule. Such interventions are in fact discretionary policies at heart. The difference is that the "rule" governs the process with occasional interventions by policy makers. Under rational expectations hypothesis such interventions must be explained to economic agents and justified in order to maintain the public trust in the system. Interventions must be infrequent with clear and transparent objectives and outcomes. This is substantially different, at least in principle, from discretionary policy, which seems to be case specific and has to be reformulated each time.

It is not clear why the discretion or the rule should be an "all or nothing" policy as earlier debates implied. After all, neither discretion nor rule would work if it is not based on economic reality and understanding. It seems that inflation targeting, although it is by implication a rule, is in fact a compromise. It establishes general guidelines without locking the guiding mechanism in a fixed position. In the "time consistency" or "dynamic consistency" literature rules are pre-committed solutions that enhance a dynamic optimization problem.[9] At first it might be difficult to gain the trust of economic agents, but it is vital to continue maintaining transparency and to follow the announced policy. It is necessary to declare under what conditions a policy rule will be pursued, changed, or discontinued.

It is possible to also identify and declare procedures and methods of transitioning form one policy rule to another. Consequently, changes in the stated policy will not be arbitrary or discretionary. There is no reason why such policy rules should be limited to monetary policy. Similar procedures can be designed and implemented for fiscal policy and even automatic stabilizers. Sometimes fiscal policies, and especially automatic stabilizers, are designed to achieve other objectives, such as social justice, in addition to their role as macroeconomic tools. It is even possible to design automatic stabilizers for the sole purpose of social justice. The extent of the influence of such policies on macroeconomic outcomes depends on the specific policy.

The notion of a policy rule solves many of the issues related to fixed rules as well as discretionary policies. In this context, the policy rule provides a somewhat automatic and predetermined gauge to determine discrepancy between the desired and actual values of key variables, such as inflation, output, the exchange rate, or the supply of money, depending on the choice of target. However, since the economic remedy to the problem is the same regardless of the detection mechanism used to determine the discrepancy, the issue of the magnitude of the variable's response to intervention still remains unsolved. For example, when the target is a specific inflation rate and the policy rule indicates there is a need to increase the interest rate since there is a positive inflation gap, it is still necessary to determine how much the interest rate needs to be increased. By associating the extent of changes in inflation targeting with the inflation gap and output gap, the need for discretion is reduced and possibly eliminated.

Taylor Rule

Inflation targeting is commonly known as the Taylor Rule. The "rule" however, is not a fixed value, as suggested by Friedman. Instead, it is designed to respond to changes in the supply of money or the short-term interest rate, which itself is governed by the fluctuations in real income and prices. The theoretical foundation of this subject stems from rational expectations hypothesis, which does not necessarily imply monetary or fiscal policies are ineffective. Rather, it suggests that because of the potency of the tools it is necessary to use them in an anticipated, consistent, and persistent manner. Inflation targeting uses modeling techniques to estimate an effective rule. Taylor[10] simulates a rational expectations model based on data from G-7 countries utilizing different monetary policy rules. He ranks the policy rules based on their performance with regard to price and output stability. He then estimates the distribution of the shocks.

The claim is that averaging inflation rates over four quarters converts the data into real values. In practice, different and often more complex smoothing techniques are employed. The determining factor in selecting a particular smoothing method is the type of data, for example, monthly versus quarterly, and the length of available data. Taylor[11] uses the value of 2% as the equilibrium real growth rate, which is close to the steady-state growth rate that is believed to be 2.2% for the United States. When inflation exceeds an arbitrary target rate, 2% in this example, the Federal Funds rate increases. Similarly, if the GDP gap exceeds an arbitrary output, also 2% in Taylor's example, the Federal Funds rate increases as well. It is easy to verify that the desired targets are matched by observing that the nominal federal funds rate is 4%.

On one hand, this "rule" is designed to respond to changes in the economy, which makes it endogenous. Thus, the magnitude of the response is based on the magnitudes of the output gap and inflation gap. On the other hand, the "rule" is not completely automatic and there is room for discretion. A major objective is to keep the rule simple. Nevertheless, the process is far from being simple. In addition to the issues raised by Friedman regarding any discretionary policy, advocates of inflation targeting such as Taylor[12] also point out that it is necessary to determine if changes in prices are temporary or permanent, and also to estimate future inflation, which requires examination of economic variables in great detail. Taylor provides additional situations where it is necessary to use discretion and provides an analysis of situations where this approach has been utilized. Here, it suffices to point out that in the aftermath of the 1987 stock market crash the Fed afforded additional reserves to the banking system to avoid a reduction in the supply of money. Taylor correctly points out that such examples and justifications are customarily used to support a discretionary policy rather than a rule. Nevertheless, Taylor argues that "policy rules have major advantages over discretion in improving economic performance."

Taylor[13] utilizes the standard deviation of the output deflator about its mean, that is, the target, as a measure of price volatility. This is a more meaningful measure of price volatility than the rate of change in price levels. Price volatility differs among industrial countries. It seems that inflation targeting is more effective when the central bank focuses on domestic economic reality rather than observing the exchange rate. Therefore, interest rates are affected by local, rather than international, factors. However, inflation targeting is more effective when the foreign exchange rate is flexible, instead of fixed or pegged. According to Taylor,[14] both the price level and real output have a direct impact on the interest rate and the empirical evidence for the United States can be summarized by the following interest rate rule:

$$r = p + .5y + .5(p - 2) + 2$$

where r is the federal funds rate, p is inflation over the previous four quarters, and y is the percent deviation of real GDP from a target. There seems to be some consensus that this original Taylor Rule is a reasonable approximation for data from various countries. The formula could be modified to accommodate other inflation rate targets, instead of 2% rate.

An equally important issue that sets policy rules apart from discretionary policy is the transition from one policy rule to another. If a policy rule never changes it could become disjoint from reality and fail to perform satisfactorily. By design, policy rules adapt to economic conditions and signal the need to change the interest rate accordingly. An important concern is that when a policy rule changes, expectations may not change, or change slowly. These are more likely when the previous policy rule lasted for a while. The longer a policy rule remains unchanged, the slower the change will be in expectations regarding the new policy rule. Therefore, when a change occurs after a prolonged stability requiring a new policy rule the formation of new expectations will be slower. In other words, it will take a while for people to correct their expectations. Thus, new policy rules must be well-publicized, explained, and transparent to assist adjustments in public expectations about the policy's objects. One particular drawback is a lack of trust in the actions or motives of the policy makers. Regardless of the approach, the issue of establishing the credibility of the new policy rule requires time. Consequently, the effect of the new policy rule may be different than the expected outcome, at least for a while. It is also possible that economic factors might be rigid and unable to adjust even if the economic agents wish to modify their behavior in response to the new policy rule. Rigidity could be due to plans, contracts, and obligations decided and committed to under the previous policy rule. Rigidity might also arise from the belief that other people are unable to modify their behavior due to lack of trust, familiarity, or acceptance of the new policy.

The degree to which rigidity causes an inability to adjust to a new policy rule depends on the length of existing contracts and obligations under the old rule, as well as the degree of skepticism about the new rule's validity or effectiveness. It could be that individuals might be incapable of changing their long-term investment. For example, a mortgage may be up to 40 years long and not many people will live to see two mortgages to maturity. However, houses can be bought and sold or refinanced. None of these actions, however, are quick, easy, or inexpensive.

A period of transition becomes necessary for two separate reasons. First, changes in factors affecting the economy change economic variables. The changes might be due to external shocks, economic bottlenecks, or shifts in expectations and objectives. Consequently, the deviation between actual and full employment output, or the output gap, as well as between the inflation rate and the target rate, can fluctuate. As a result, the policy rule will indicate a necessary change in policy, such as raising or lowering the interest rate. Thus, a transition becomes necessary. This type of change and the pursing transition are easier to explain to the public and do not require justification of the objectives of the policy rule since the policy objectives have not changed. Another source of the need for change, and thus transition, is in the context where there are shifts in the objectives of the policy rule. These shifts are often due to changes in political power, which is an ongoing battle among special interest groups and different factions both within and outside of the government. These changes could cause a shift in the economic fortunes of different groups since strengthening of one special group or ideology is always associated with changes in the status quo. In general, the economy is in Pareto equilibrium. Consequently, it is not possible to improve the welfare of a person or a group without reducing the welfare of another person or group. The winners of the political struggle and their constituents will gain and the beneficiaries of the previous policy rule will lose. Other groups and special interests will gain or lose based on compatibility of their objectives and fortunes with the winners and losers of such political forces.

Fiscal Policy Applications

Earlier, it was stated that inflation targeting can be applied to fiscal policy as well. The concept and the purpose are the same but the tools are different. The interest rate is a monetary policy tool and cannot be modified through fiscal actions. However, fiscal policy can change the unemployment benefit. The change can be in the amount of pay per period or the length of the period itself. Changes in the rates of payment are not as common as changes in the duration of the unemployment benefits. The changes must be approved by the Congress, which could slow down the process, especially if the majority in one or the other chamber of Congress and the Office of the President are of different political persuasions. Based on the rational expectations hypothesis the consequences could also be different depending on the public's perception of whether the changes are transitory or permanent. All statements from legislators with regard to the nature of such a change play a key role in influencing the formation of public expectations.

SECTION IV

The Evidence

CHAPTER 11

Empirical Evidence Supporting Monetary Policy

The previous ten chapters provide a minute fraction of what needs to be said about monetary theory and its policy implications. Scholars have been writing about monetary theory, policy, or both for over two centuries. The focus of the present book has been broad and conceptual. For example, the detailed analytical requirements of applying rational expectation hypothesis have been bypassed in order to explain what it means and what its implications are.

Economic theories are formed to explain the economic behavior of humans. There is no economic theory without a human element. It is important to validate economic theories through empirical analysis to provide evidence of the correctness of the theory. Theories are based on assumptions that are believed to be reasonable, meaningful, or axiomatically obvious. For example, it is believed that more is preferred to less on the grounds that if something is desirable at all, more of it should be more desirable. This statement is simplistic in that it will only apply to a limited range of behavior. For example, although more shoes are preferred to fewer shoes, conceivably there is a point where one has too many shoes, such as when there is no more room in the house to keep the shoes. Another example is the overconsumption of food. In chemistry, it is said that every substance becomes a toxin at some dose. Many young people discover this reality after having too much to drink.

Sometimes the evidence may not support the theory because the theory is incorrect, or because the assumptions of the theory are not met. No one necessarily behaves according to the assumptions of a theory, or according to the logic of the theory. Theories are acceptable as long as there is sufficient evidence that they can explain reality; recall the walking leaves of Friedman. Sometimes the theories fail to explain new realities because of changes to the economy or economic agents' behavior. In this chapter we provide some of the more compelling evidence in support of monetary policy as well as some evidence that reveals its shortcomings. We will avoid a laundry list of articles testing the validities of theories and assumptions since that would take several volumes and is of dubious benefit. Instead, attention is focused on a few major works and the overall state of our understanding of the role of monetary policy and its instruments in the economy.

With regard to discretionary policy, its effectiveness is important in addition to the correctness of a theory. In order for the monetary policy to be effective, it must have the correct and anticipated outcome in a timely fashion. The policy must yield its desired outcome in less time than the length of a half a phase of an economic cycle, otherwise the economy moves to the next phase of the cycle and the policy becomes ineffective and most likely harmful. The shorter the outside lag of a policy, the more preferred is the policy. Unless the policy is automatically activated, it is necessary that the sum of the inside and outside lag to be less than half of a phase of the cycle. It is also necessary to know the magnitude of the expected response to a given amount of change in the policy instrument. Finally, it is necessary to be able to determine the position of the economy on the business cycle. Without having this information and knowledge, it would not be possible to use monetary policy to achieve a desired outcome.

Since there are different instruments at the disposal of monetary authorities the answer to the above questions must be determined for all instruments. When dealing with multiple instruments, it is also necessary to determine which one is more effective, or appropriate, for a particular situation.

Effectiveness of Monetary Theory

Friedman and Schwartz[1] provide one of the most comprehensive empirical works on monetary theory. The work is a deliberate set of analyses to support Friedman's effort to revive the classical quantity theory. Friedman's work involves numerous theoretical improvements to the classical monetary theory that incorporate components from other areas, including Keynesian theory, into the quantity theory to enable it to more effectively explain the economy. One example is the inclusion of the interest rate in the demand for money. He also incorporates new ideas that have no precedence in the classical quantity theory, or other theories, such as the permanent income hypothesis, in order to cast doubt on fiscal theory, improve the explanatory power of the monetary theory, obtain a more general theory, and to provide more reliable prediction of the outcome of changes in monetary instruments.

Friedman's[2] modern quantity theory expresses the demand for real balances as a function of permanent income, expected return on bonds, expected returns on money, expected return on stocks, and expected inflation. The important points of the theory are the inclusion of the interest rate and the use of permanent income. Friedman and Schwartz[3] explain fluctuations of yields on several assets that are alternatives to holding money as economizing on money balances, evidenced by graphing data from 1929 to 1960. They point out that between 1946 and 1960 the velocity of money increased sharply while the interest rate was rising. They attribute the increase in interest rate to a shift in expectations; the change in the interest rate causes increase in velocity. This hypothesis sharply contrasts with the advocates of the classical quantity theory, who did not include the interest rate in the money demand function and assumed a constant velocity.

Friedman[4] depicts per capita demand for real balances as a direct function of per capita permanent net national product and an inverse function of the permanent price level. A simple version of this model is employed in Friedman and Meiselman,[5] where demand for real balances is expressed as a function of net national product only. Their conclusion is that money is a luxury. Ando and Modigliani[6] apply a definition of money, both narrower and wider, to the same dataset and conclude that money behaves more like a normal than a luxury good. A coefficient of numeral one, or close to it, would imply a proportional increase in demand with respect to changes in income. Whether money is a luxury or a normal good has some economic importance, but the more important fact is that when modifying the definition of money causes such a drastic change in the conclusions reached about the impact of increasing the money supply, it casts doubt on the role of money demand. In spite of ample empirical evidence, Tobin and Swan[7] question the importance of the supply of money because of the lack of theory, yet they acknowledge that Friedman and Schwartz's[8] permanent income hypothesis is testable. In specific, they question the use of prices in an empirical model of the permanent income hypothesis because prices are not exogenous. Instead, they should be estimated endogenously using structural equations. Tobin and Swan also find the errors of the model contain serial correlations. They find that interest rates can provide an explanation for the pro-cyclical movement of velocity with respect to the demand for money. Their final conclusion is that Friedman and Schwartz's[9] model of permanent income hypothesis fails to outperform a naïve model using the previous year as the best estimate of the present outcome.

Friedman and Schwartz[10] state that changes in the money supply have been exogenous in the United States, and there is a stable association between changes in the stock of money and economic activities, money income, and prices. They neither establish nor claim a causal relationship between the supply of money and other variables. In fact, they actually warn the readers not to make such a conclusion. Nevertheless, they conclude: "Changes in the money stock are therefore a consequence as well as an independent source of changes in money income and prices, though, since they occur, they produce still further effects on income and prices . . . this is the generalization supported by our evidence." However, Friedman has repeatedly stated that in the long run, "money does not matter," indicating that only real variables, and not monetary factors, can change real income.

Friedman[11] declares that inflation is a monetary phenomenon. He points out that prices were stable from 1867 to 1960 except for the periods immediately after the two World Wars. During the same period mild contractions occurred every four years on average with six severe recessions, which coincided with monetary contractions, especially the Great Depression. Each of these is used to demonstrate the effectiveness of the monetary policy, and hence, its importance. Friedman and Meiselman[12] find that the supply of money explains consumption better than autonomous expenditures.

Definition

Autonomous expenditures are expenditures that do not depend on income or production. Each sector of consumption, investment, government expenditures, and net exports is assumed to have a component that is a function of income or production and a portion that is not.

Autonomous expenditures are exogenous to the model since they are not affected by the internal forces of the economy, with the exception of money according to Friedman and Meiselman.[13] In the case of consumption this variable reflects the subsistence consumption of the Keynesian consumption function. Friedman and Meiselman[14] posit that the part of consumption that depends on income or production responds to the internal forces of the economy. Yet the autonomous parts are more receptive to changes in the supply of money than to changes in income. However, this does not necessarily mean that changes in the supply of money would not affect income levels, or production, and consequently the endogenous component of consumption.

Friedman and Meiselman run regressions on six different formulations of consumption.

$$C = \alpha_1 + \beta_1 A_1$$
$$C = \alpha_2 + \delta_2 M_2$$
$$C = \alpha_3 + \beta_3 A + \gamma_3 P_3$$
$$C = \alpha_4 + \delta_4 + \gamma_4 P_4$$
$$C = \alpha_5 + \beta_5 A + \delta_5 M_5$$
$$C = \alpha_6 + \beta_6 A + \delta_6 M + \gamma_6 P_6$$

where C is consumption in current dollars (durables, nondurables, and services); A is autonomous expenditure in current dollars (net private domestic investment, government deficit on income and product account, and the net foreign balance); M is money supply (currency in public circulation; adjusted demand deposits, and commercial bank time deposits); and P is the consumer price index.

The models are different versions of the same consumption function in terms of autonomous expenditures. Equation 1 includes only the autonomous expenditures, while equations 3, 5, and 6 add other variables, one at a time. Equation 2 has the money supply as the only independent variable, while equations 4 and 6 add other variables to the model. A main problem with this approach is that only one of the models can "theoretically" be correct, which makes the others mis-specified, causing different degrees of problems. They find out that the coefficients for the money supplies in different models are larger than the coefficients for autonomous expenditures, and that the models with the supply of money have higher coefficients of determination. Neither conclusion is really an indication of the superiority of the model. Hester[15] questions their use of a narrow definition of autonomous expenditures; especially, the exclusion of taxes. He points out that the omission of taxes from the discussion implies the balanced budget multiplier is zero. He also questions the wisdom of using such simplistic models with different variables.

Ando and Modigliani[16] point out that simple correlation does not mean anything when there are multiple variables that affect the dependent variable. Exclusion of relevant variables from a model results in omitted variable bias.[17] They also question the treatment of war years. The issue in dealing with "special or unusual" data points is a problem afflicting most of the studies of the effectiveness of monetary and fiscal policies. Ando and Modigliani[18] add "currency outside banks plus adjusted demand deposits, plus time deposits in commercial banks" as explanatory variables to Friedman's and Meiselman's model,[19] and obtain substantially superior results. They also repeat the same analysis by excluding the years during World War II and obtain a better result than Friedman and Meiselman.

DePrano and Mayer[20] question the use of simple versions of fiscal and monetary theories. They point out that a theory is valid in part because of its requirements or assumptions. They provide the following example; "Let us compare two theories, one asserting that heavy objects drop faster than light ones, and one asserting that they fall equally fast. If we take simple versions of these two theories which make no assumption about the absence of air pressure, and test them by dropping a lead ball and a feather from a tower, the theory that heavy objects fall faster will surely emerge the winner." In terms of economics they claim the predictive power of Keynesian models changes when consumption is assumed to be a function of net national product instead of disposable income. They argue that "autonomous expenditures give an extreme version of the Keynesian theory" and that using the "money stock gives an extreme version of the quantity theory."

In the simple versions of fiscal and monetary theory many variables are assumed to be exogenous, while in reality they are not. For example, the supply of money is assumed to be set by monetary authorities, and thus, by definition is inelastic, which is depicted as a vertical line. Although the process by which the monetary authorities set the supply of money has some degree of "human subjectivity," nevertheless, it is far from being arbitrary or capricious. The Fed reacts to the economic realities in determining the supply of money. It is possible that the supply of money is set to achieve a particular outcome, such as to increase employment or to decrease inflation, but these are not arbitrary either. Except by mistake, the Fed will not attempt to lower inflation during economic downturns, or to increase employment while there is shortage of labor. Theoretically, the supply of money is endogenous and is not set arbitrarily. DePrano and Mayer[21] also point out that it is not acceptable to define independent variables for testing a hypothesis using the hypothesis itself, which they claim is what Friedman and Meiselman[22] have done in defining autonomous expenditures. By modifying the variables and including additional variables, DePrano and Mayer[23] conclude that the Keynesian theory performs well. Changing the length of observation also changes the outcome, hence reducing the explanatory power of the model.

The exception is the period 1929–1939, which they claim is solely because of the year 1929; the elimination of which results in compliance with other periods. At first, it seemed that the evidence is overwhelmingly in favor of monetary policy. Closer examination of the evidence casts doubt on this conclusion. The choice of models, variables, and the length of observations seems to make a difference. This last issue is of greatest concern. When estimation and prediction depends on a particular period the corresponding theory is not universal. It can be proven that for a sample of size "n," a model with "$n-1$" variables will provide perfect fit. More generally, by trial and error one can obtain a statistically significant relationship between dependent and independent variables for a given set of data. However, once the data changes the model loses its power. Robust models are not affected by minor changes in data, such as adding new observations.

Economists do not know what to do with "exceptional" observations. The severity of the Great Depression is a good example of this point; an observation this extreme has occurred only once in the past two hundred years or so. Should its data be included or excluded from analysis? Should all recessions be excluded as well or should the model be capable of explaining all observations, including the exceptionally different ones? Studies of the effectiveness of monetary and fiscal policies obtain widely different outcomes by changing which observations are included, or which statistical procedures are implemented. The choice of statistical modeling is based on the nature of assumptions about the economy and the conduct of humans. The choice of variables is also important.

One of the main problems of using statistical analysis to prove the validity of one theory or another is that the statistical significance of chosen variables does not prove validity of a theory, let alone disprove the validity of a rival theory. Economic variables are correlated, and every economic factor is affected by other factors; available data in most cases are crude proxies for theoretically required variables, and the true functional form of the relationship is unknown. Statistical models are not valid instruments to prove the correctness of economic theories. The 1960s and part of the 1970s witnessed numerous studies on monetary as well as fiscal policy effectiveness, where different formulations of the theory with different sets of variables produced different results in favor of one, or the other, rival theory. Although the practice is useless in settling theoretical arguments, it nevertheless exposes the shortcomings and advantages of each ideology behind the theories, which has resulted in improved economic understandings and stronger theories.

Nominal income is determined by the supply of money, which in turn is a function of numerous factors, as evidenced by Friedman and Schwartz.[24] Regardless of the sources of increase in the money supply, Friedman[25] claims that its relationship has been stable with other economic variables, especially the velocity of money. However, Moore[26] points out that the stock of money accounts for only 30% of variations in velocity when annual data are used. When quarterly data are used the explanatory power drops to 11%. Hamburger[27] demonstrates that the velocity of money is stable when using the M_2 definition and that the M_2 supply of money is not affected by the autonomous investment expenditures.

Empirical Evidence for Austrian Business Cycle Theory

A major tenant of the Austrian business cycle theory is that monetary shocks disturb relative prices. They alter profit rates by shifting the term structure of interest rates. When resource users respond to these changes a cyclical pattern of real income emerges. A primary objective of empirical studies of this school is to determine whether the effects of price changes, which are induced by changes in the supply of money, are sufficient to trigger a business cycle. Hayek's theory failed to gain support, in part due to overwhelming acceptance of the alternative solution offered by Keynes. Consequently, few empirical tests of the theory are available, most of which are post-1970s, when Keynesian theory began to fail to explain the economic reality of the time.

According to Mises,[28] one problem limiting empirical study of the Austrian school's theories is the impracticality of measurement. One possible source of this problem is the need to aggregate microeconomic data into macroeconomic data to be able to test hypotheses about business cycles. The empirical evidence is sparse and mostly non-analytical. The advocates of the Austrian school seem to find evidence of imminent recession if they find evidence of badly matched capital stock instead of too much capital, which one might consider as evidence of overinvestment. One possible example that might support the theory is presented by Summers,[29] where he claims that the U.S. recession of 2001, similar to the recession of Japan in the 1980s, was caused by excess credit, rather than excess demand. However, he does not provide any analytical evidence for his claim.

Wainhouse[30] provides a rare empirical study of Hayek's theory. He studies the effect of changes in the supply of money on interest rates and the change in the ratio of prices of consumer goods relative to that of producer goods, using monthly data from 1959 to 1981 for the United States. To demonstrate the direction of the relationship he utilizes the Granger causality test. Whether finding evidence that changes in supply of money affects the variables in the study indicates that an increase in the money supply causes recession or not is not determined in the article. However, it is evident that the Austrian theory of the business cycle and its claim that expansionary monetary policy causes recession is not well supported by empirical research.

Empirical Evidence for Rational Expectations Hypothesis

Contrary to the case of Austrian business cycle theory, the evidence in support of the rational expectations hypothesis is abundant. Lucas[31] points out that Hume's discussions about the effect of money hinges on "the way in which the change is effected." Lucas questions Hume's argument that the "first recipients" of an increase in the supply of money (i.e., gold) have an advantage over others, since they obtain it first and can buy goods at existing prices before they rise in response to an increase in the supply of money, which occurs exogenously. Lucas wonders why the rest of the population does not realize the inevitable increase in prices that would result from an increase in the supply of money. The importance of this point for Lucas is that Hume "deduced the quantity theory of money" by assuming "that people act rationally and that this fact is reflected in market-determined quantities and prices." The same rationality assumption implies that people should also know that prices will increase in response to an increase in supply of money. Lucas points out that averaging data over time eliminates short run fluctuations, and thus, leaves the long run association. He provides a graph from McCandless and Weber[32] that plots the average annual inflation rates for 110 countries over 30 years against their average annual growth rate of $M2$. The data are distributed closely about the 45-degree line indicating a strong relationship. They also report that the correlation when M_1 is used is 0.96, and it is 0.92 when M_2 is used. The correlation when M_2 is used is 0.96 and 0.99 for OECD and Latin American countries, respectively. On the other hand, there is no association between the growth rate of money and real output. Thus, they establish a link between the supply of money and inflation in the long run and refute any relationship between the supply of money and real variables, such as output, in the long run. The short run relationship between money supply and prices are discussed by Friedman and Schwartz,[33] as explained earlier in the chapter. This relationship is more evident in the cases of recessions within the United States. However, Sargent[34] demonstrates that the same relationship does not exist for European countries, although the magnitudes of the reduction in the supply of money in those cases were much larger than those in the United States. A determining factor is whether the specific monetary shock to the system is anticipated or not.

Sargent and Wallace[35] demonstrate that the rational expectations hypothesis is consistent with the observed relationship between inflation and the creation of money and propose that the latter causes the former.

They also find that there exists "substantial evidence of feedback from inflation to money creation, with markedly less feedback from money creation to inflation."

Acemoglu and Scott[36] demonstrate that consumption and consumer confidence are correlated and conclude that consumers are able to predict future income as the rational expectations permanent income hypothesis would indicate. Nevertheless, they also conclude that "the confidence indicator is also a leading indicator for consumption, contradicting the rational expectations permanent income hypothesis."

Empirical Evidence for Inflation Targeting

Empirical evidence about inflation targeting is vast. Numerous studies test the use of inflation targeting in single countries, as well as regions. The majority of results are favorable and supportive of the practice. Even in countries where there is no stated inflation targeting policy, such as the United States, there is ample evidence that the outcome of prolonged low inflation can be attributed to the pursuit of an inflation targeting policy by the central bank.

It is not surprising that the original Taylor Rule fits the data for the United States well because the rule is an empirical estimation of the federal funds rate. Although the Federal Reserve Bank does not have an announced inflation targeting policy, the moderate to low inflation of recent history and Taylor's empirical evidence indicate that the Fed is actually pursuing an inflation targeting policy of some kind. Since 1993 there has been ample evidence of the existence of inflation targeting and application of the Taylor rule in numerous countries. Bryant, Hooper, and Mann[37] provide a comparative study of nine multi-country models based on different monetary rule policies. The models were based on gaps between actual and targeted values of the supply of money, foreign exchange rates, inflation, output, or some combination of these gaps. Naghshpour and St. Marie[38] find evidence for the applicability of the Taylor Rule in Europe, and Naghshpour and St. Marie[39] confirm similar findings for several Latin American countries. The performances of different models are different as well as the performances of the same model on different countries. It seems that policy rules which focus on the foreign exchange rate or the supply of money do not perform as well as those based on an inflation gap or output gap, although the effectiveness of these models is not uniform either. Therefore, the short-term interest rate is a more effective policy instrument than alternative tools. The economic theory is the same as ever; namely, when the price level, output, or both are above the targeted rate, it is necessary to increase the interest rate. When those values are below the target the opposite correction is necessary. The wider the income or output gap the greater the magnitude of the change in the short-term interest rate. It would be wise not to attempt to "tweak" the system by constantly changing the short-term interest rate when output and inflation gaps are small. It is vital to choose a reasonable inflation or output target. A wise choice would be the full employment level of output and a modest rate of price increases. In practice, the accepted norm is about 2% inflation and the best estimate of the full employment level of output is its trend value.

CHAPTER 12

Conclusion

As in other sciences, economic theories depend on the assumptions that are used in their formation. Even the simplest economic concepts are based on specific assumptions. For example, the downward sloping demand curve is based on the assumption that the good is not a Giffen good. One might consider cases such as Giffen goods as exceptions to the rule, which exist in every branch of science. However, attempting to test the validity of a theory without consideration of its assumptions is misleading. Recall from Chapter 11 the importance of assuming the existence of a vacuum and a lack of friction in the physics theory that claims all objects fall at the same rate. Examinations of economic theories without regard to the underlying assumptions are also misleading. In addition, economic events and factors that affect them are stochastic or random and are therefore subject to probabilistic outcomes.

Theories in many disciplines contradict each other and economic theories are no exception. This is not to say that there are no theories that are accepted by the majority, if not all, economists. One example is that the supply curve is upward sloping. Even in cases when consensus exists, the slope or the degree of responsiveness of the phenomenon to its determining factors might be disputed by different theories belonging to different schools of thought. Customarily, it is expected that theories be logical, plausible, coherent, and internally consistent. Otherwise, the theory is easily rejected. The differences in the outcomes of theories stems from differences in their assumptions and which influential factors are incorporated into them. The presence of competing theories with drastically different consequences is common in fields where experimental studies are either not possible or impractical. For example, it is not possible to conduct an experiment in astronomy by creating several universes and subjecting them to different treatments to test the validity of theories pertaining to the birth and development of universe.

Anytime a theory involves human subjects, it is more difficult, or in some cases impossible, to conduct tests based on experimental design because of ethical considerations and the willpower of human subjects. For example, in order to examine the consequence of an increase in the supply of money, it is necessary to have a control group within the economy and at least one treatment group, where the latter is subject to a change in the supply of money while the former is not; all other aspects of the lives of the two groups are kept identical. One might be tempted to study a single country over several years and compare the outcome of an increase in the supply of money by comparing the years before and after the change. Unfortunately, this will not work because the supply of money is constantly changing in every economy; therefore, there are no before and after cases to be studied. Sometimes a major change in the supply of money occurs due to a dramatic situation or a significant policy change; but by virtue of being an exception, it is not possible to test any of the existing theories on the supply of money using such a change because the theories are for the general case and not the exception. Note that it is not possible to test a theory about the general conduct and response of an economy using an exceptional situation. To complicate the situation, we know that human beings respond differently to an increase in the supply of money depending on their belief of whether or not the change is temporary, as explained by the permanent income hypothesis. Furthermore, it is necessary to assure that the assumptions of each theory are met before one can conduct the experiment. In fields of study that involve human beings and deal with a multitude of factors, it is impossible in most cases, if not all, to control for all relevant factors as required in experimental design. Recall how the outcome of the experiment on the law of falling objects pivots on the assumption of a lack of atmospheric pressure. In other words, the law is valid only in a vacuum. In studies involving human beings the influencing factors are numerous and customarily impossible to control by the research.

Another factor that complicates testing the validity of theories in economics is that everything in economics is related to everything else. If there is a general rule in economics, it is that there is no general rule. This statement is more valid for empirical evidence than theory. Theories, and thus models, depend on *ceteris paribus*, or "other things being equal."

For example, an increase in supply of money is said to reduce its price, which is the interest rate, provided other things remain the same as before the increase in the supply of money. However, it is possible that when the supply of money increases the velocity of money changes instead of the interest rate. The outcome of this increase in the money supply will be different depending on whether the velocity increases, remains constant, or decreases. Note that the velocity of money is assumed to remain constant when the supply of money changes. Yet, a change in velocity is certainly possible, both because of economic reasons as well as the fact that different people might interpret the causes and the consequences of changes in the supply of money differently at different times, and hence respond differently to the same change in the supply of money, thus, causing alternative outcomes.

One way of dealing with assumptions in econometrics is to include the variables that are believed to have an impact on the response variable in the model. These variables are also called control variables but they are not the same as the control variable in an experimental design. In an experimental design study subjects are selected according to a predetermined procedure. Some, at random, are not treated at all while the others are subjected to different treatments of interest. Since the original subjects are chosen at random the averages of grouping different subjects should differ from each other only by a magnitude no larger than what can be attributed to random error. Consequently, any difference between the control group and the treatment group(s) can be attributed to treatment(s) only. The control variables in econometrics, however, are not controlled for anything at all. They are observations that were subject to the same economic forces that affect the response variable. Their inclusion in the model accounts for some of the changes in the response variable; thus, it is claimed that the model has controlled for the effects of these variables. Therefore, the control variables in econometric modeling are considerably different than those in experimental design.

It is important to restate the fact that the control variables in econometric models are also affected by the same forces in the economy that affect the response variable. Furthermore, other exogenous variables in an econometric model are also subject to the same forces and are correlated with the so-called control variables, causing multicollinearity. One consequence of multicollinearity is that the actual effect of an exogenous variable is not simply the magnitude of its coefficient. Consequently, its true impact on the response variable cannot be isolated and determined independently from other exogenous variables. Another issue caused by multicollinearity is that some variables which are expected to affect the response variable based on theory, may in fact fail to be statistically significant in the presence of another variable or variables with which they are correlated. For example, the variable representing education might be statistically insignificant in explaining income in the presence of a gender or race variable. On the other hand, the exclusion of a gender and race variable would make the education variable statistically significant. However, not controlling for gender or race is not defendable since a test of equality of means of incomes for different races and genders will indicate significant differences exist between them. Furthermore, excluding a variable that actually belongs to the model causes misspecification and estimation bias. It is also possible that different combinations of variables will explain the response variable to different degrees, one of which will be higher and seem to be better. However, changes in the data points used in the analysis will most likely change the explanatory power of the model. In other words, when new data becomes available the inclusion of this new data could yield a different "best model" and possibly a different set of explanatory variables.

The presence of multicollinearity is a serious problem for economic studies because having the correct signs and magnitudes of coefficients is essential in determining the validity of theories. Since under multicollinearity the coefficients are meaningless by themselves, placing too much stock in the magnitudes of the coefficients would be misguided. Furthermore, the inclusion or exclusion of other variables affects the coefficients of variables of interest, which exacerbates the difficulty of determining which theory is supported or refuted by the empirical analysis. The presence of multicollinearity is one explanation for the existence of numerous empirical works in many areas of economics, especially in studies that address fiscal and monetary theory, where different sets of variables are used to explain a given theoretical question.

In the presence of multicollinearity, different sets of collinear variables are capable of providing similar degrees of explanatory power for a model.

Consequently, different studies are able to present reasonable estimations of various outcomes using different sets of variables. A common problem among studies afflicted with multicollinearity is that they provide poor forecasts and that they are not robust. Consequently, empirical studies using different sets of variables, periods of data, or both provide contradictory conclusions. One way to check for robustness of the results is to add new data when it becomes available, or to delete data that has become too old. Older data are expected to have less impact as time passes, which justifies their exclusion. The inclusion or exclusion of new data should not change the coefficients by much. Specifically, the significance or lack there off, and the sign of the coefficient, should remain the same. In economics, changes in the magnitude of coefficients should not change their elasticity, which would imply a substantially different outcome. For example, a small change in a coefficient could change the perception a good from being a normal good to a luxury or an inferior good.

Theories are broad while empirical models must be specific. For example, in the quantity theory the quantity of real money multiplied by velocity is equal to the value of transactions in an economy in one year, as depicted by the equation of exchange. This theory does not specify the particular variable that should be used for money. In practice, there are several variables that could be used to represent money, such as M1, M2, and M3; only one of these alternative variables can be used in an empirical study. Consequently, at least three different models can be formulated, one for each of the three response variables, to test the merit of the quantity theory. One would expect that the results should be similar; however, in reality, the set of variables that explain M2 need not and in fact do not explain M1 or M3 well. There are many alternative options for each of independent variables as well. Assume that there are k variables that are believed to explain a single response variable. Let each of these variables have n_i alternative choices. For example, in the case of human capital one can use the median years of schooling, percentage of people over 25 with high school, baccalaureate, masters, or PhD degrees, average number of schooling, and so forth. The number of alternative models that can be utilized will be a staggering number obtained by:

$$N = n_1 \times n_2 \times \ldots \times n_k$$

Assuming $k = 5$, $n_1 = 4$, $n_2 = 3$, $n_3 = 6$, $n_4 = 4$, and $n_5 = 5$, the number of different models that can be established will be:

$$N = 4 \times 3 \times 6 \times 4 \times 5 = 1440$$

The above number is obtained by assuming that all the models use all the variables. In practice, any subset of available variables can be used, and usually there are much more than five variables that are considered relevant in many economic studies.

The practice of having different numbers of variables in models that are used to test a particular theory introduces the concern of misspecification. Misspecification occurs when there are too many or too few variables than the correct number of variables. When variables that belong to a model are excluded the type of misspecification is known as the problem of omitted variables. When there are omitted variables the coefficients of the included variables are biased, which means that the expected value of the estimated coefficient is not equal to the true parameter that is estimated. In the presence of multicollinearity the particular set of variables that provides the "best fit" need not include all the theoretically expected factors or control variables, which makes it difficult to determine if the model is mis-specified, and if so, what the extent of misspecification is and whether it is the case of an omitted variable or the inclusion of an irrelevant variable.

A review of the literature reveals that numerous studies have a myriad of variables. For example, DePrano and Mayer[1] use 20 different definitions of autonomous variables alone. Of course this article is not an exception; although many articles might use fewer definitions of a particular variable, the use of different combinations of multiple variables is common in most studies. The practice of applying numerous tests using the same data causes another problem. The problem is similar to the issues that arise in multiple comparisons in experimental design studies, when the averages of many variables are compared for equality. In studies where the hypothesis that all variables are equal is rejected it is necessary to conduct pairwise comparisons, to identify which averages are the same and which ones are different. It can be shown that in the cases of repeated tests using the same data the probability of type I error increases to a much higher level than intended. Type I error is the error of rejecting the null hypothesis when the null hypothesis is in fact true. It is necessary to divide the desired probability of type I error by the number of comparisons and use the much smaller probability as the basis of inference. The procedure is commonly known as the Bonferroni correction.

Another problem that afflicts studies of fiscal and monetary theory involves the nature of assumptions, both in theoretical and empirical studies. An important example is the assumption of the exogeneity of the supply of money. In many theories and empirical research the supply of money is depicted as a vertical line, indicating it is exogenous. There are two justifications for this assumption. First, the Fed can set the supply of money at any level that it desires. Second, in the short run the supply of money cannot be changed, at least not by a noticeable amount. The second justification might be plausible if there are rigidities in the market. However, the money market is one of the more responsive sectors of the economy, if not the quickest to respond to changes in the market. The response of the money market can be very rapid, especially if expectations have been heightened due to repeated use of discretionary policies, as set forth by the rational expectations hypothesis.

The first justification is even less realistic. The Fed employs numerous economists to gauge economic conditions in order to be able to determine the appropriate amount of supply of money. The members of Board of Governors of the Fed are appointed for 14-year terms to shield them against retaliation by the executive branch of the government. Therefore, there is less chance that the Board would arbitrarily set the supply of money under political pressure or due to a lack of knowledge about the economy. The supply of money also depends on the amount of money created by the banking system, which is controlled through the reserve requirement and the overnight interest rate, both of which are determined by the Fed. It is plausible for the conduct of the banking system to be endogenous to the system and to depend on economic forces. For example, after the 2008 recession in the United States the lowering of the interest rate to around 0% by the Fed could not induce banks to lend more money, nor for the public to borrow more. The power of the Fed to "control" the supply of money is similar to the power of parents in controlling their children; the influence is high and strong but not ultimate.

Attempts by the central bank to set the interest rate at its equilibrium level fails because the central bank of a country does not know how to determine the equilibrium interest rate any more than economists in a centrally planned economy would.

There are several obstacles that limit the effectiveness of fiscal and monetary policies. First, it is difficult to determine the exact position of the economy on a business cycle, in part due to the lag in collecting and analyzing the relevant data. Second, after determining the gap between the target and the actual state of the economy, it is difficult to prescribe the correct dose of the instrument. The exact relationship between policy instruments and economic outcomes are not known precisely. Third, legislating and incorporating the prescribed solution takes time, especially if it involves major decisions such as changing taxes or national debt; this is the "inside lag." Fourth, the length of time for realization of the full effect of policy instruments on the economy is not known, and evidence suggests that its variance is substantial; this is the "outside lag." Fifth, the reaction of economic agents to a particular change in policy instrument is not always the same and depends on different economic conditions, as well as how often the policy instrument has been utilized before, the state of the economy, the political climate of the nation, and the expectations of economic agents. These issues convinced Milton Friedman to recommend a constant growth rate for money in lieu of applying discretionary fiscal and/or monetary policies. It is possible that the effectiveness of policy instruments cannot be determined and that their use only exacerbates economic fluctuations. The evidence indicates that outcomes of policy decisions can be forecasted; however, the quality of such forecasts is not satisfactory. This indicates that the current state of the art techniques for diagnosing economic problems and prescribing their solutions are not adequate. The solution to the problem is to utilize fiscal and monetary tools cautiously, and with full transparency. The process of improving analytical capabilities should continue until reasonable forecasts could be made of the outcomes of different policies. There is no known solution for the problem when the inherent variances of different stages of the process are substantial.

As noted above, numerous issues determine the final estimate or forecast in an empirical study of fiscal or monetary policy. Variations in modeling, variables, length of period under study, and choice of what should be declared as unusual cases, and therefore be excluded from the data set, as well as a host of other factors, such as the frequency of wielding a policy, recent history of policy uses, and expectations of economic agents, affect the magnitudes of coefficients in econometric models, as well as their statistical significance. This in turn might signal the effectiveness, or lack thereof, of fiscal or monetary policy. While hardliners of the fiscal and monetary camps might argue that one or the other policy is effective or ineffective, the majority of economists would argue that both policies are important, to some extent. Middle of the road economists might argue the point that one or the other policy is more effective, thus, making the argument an issue of the degree of effectiveness, as in the live debate of Milton Friedman and Walter Heller on November 14, 1968, during the Seventh Annual Arthur K. Salomon Lecture at the New York University, even though both presenters were considered to have orthodox views in their respective beliefs. The statement of Alfred Marshall about the importance of supply or demand might be useful in response to the question of the effectiveness of fiscal and monetary policy. Marshall resembled the effectiveness of supply and demand to the cutting ability of a pair of scissors; where the combined actions of both blades are necessary to cut. In the case of fiscal and monetary policy it is possible to exercise one without the other one. The history since the 1930s indicates that pure fiscal or monetary policy without the presence of the other is rare, if it ever existed. In modern economies, both fiscal and the monetary policies are utilized, although not necessarily to the same extent, or simultaneously, to achieve governments' economic, social, and political objectives. The degree of utilization of one policy or the other is reflective of the normative values of policy makers and economists in charge of the appropriate institutions, and often their constituents. The discussions in this book and the empirical evidence indicate that neither policy can be implemented with scientific precision and the assurance of a specific outcome. An effective approach would be to utilize all the available tools to achieve the desired objectives. At a minimum, this will allow the use of a specific instrument to be more effective, even with a lower dosage.

Some economic objectives are similar. For example the objective of increasing output, or GDP, is the same as reducing unemployment.

A reduction in unemployment increases output, but the same outcome could be achieved by increasing output, which would reduce unemployment. To achieve either objective, the more effective method is the use of expansionary fiscal or monetary policy, notwithstanding the argument that discretionary policy is ineffective. In this regard, fiscal and monetary policies are similar. However, the complete impacts of the two policies are not identical in all aspects. In addition to an increase in output and a reduction in unemployment, the outcome of an expansionary fiscal policy is that the interest rate will also increase. However, for an expansionary monetary policy, the increase in output and reduction in unemployment are accompanied by a reduction in the interest rate. An increase in the interest rate benefits lenders, while a decrease in the interest rate is beneficial to the borrowers. The objectives of increasing output and reducing unemployment are accomplished by both polices, but different groups of people benefit from the change in the interest rate, depending on whether fiscal or monetary policy is utilized to achieve these objectives. Incentives exist to influence the government's choice of policy for the same objective of increasing GDP or reducing unemployment via the policy most favorable to a particular constituency or special interest group. Here too, the rule is the same as in production theory. As long as the marginal cost is less than the marginal benefit, it is sensible to incur the cost.

In practice, and due to the influence of different constituents, governments utilize both fiscal and monetary policies jointly. In the case of the previous example, joint applications of expansionary fiscal and monetary policies will moderate their impact on the interest rate. The advantage, in addition to accommodating different constituents for political gain, is a reduction in the volatility of the interest rate which in turn serves to stabilize the economy and improve the ability of economic agents to forecast changes in the interest rate.

Monetary Policy—Glossary of Terms

Adaptive expectations mean that expectations change gradually and incrementally.

Autonomous expenditures are expenditures that do not depend on income or production. Each sector of consumption, investment, government expenditures, and net exports is assumed to have a component, which is a function of income or production and a portion that is not.

Aggregate demand is the sum of all demands by all sectors.

Balanced budget multiplier is the multiplier when changes in government expenditures and taxes are equal.

Barter is the exchange of one thing for another, when neither good is "money."

Comparative statics analysis compares two static equilibria without concern about how the market moves from one equilibrium point to another.

Crowding out refers to increase in the interest rate as a result of expansionary fiscal policy.

Deadweight loss is the loss of welfare as a result of government intervention or departures from resource allocation that would have prevailed under perfectly competitive market for any reason or by any means.

Derived demand is a demand for a product when its use does not provide direct utility. The product is demanded because it is used in production of other goods or services that provide direct utility.

Discretionary policy refers to active government intervention in economic matters via fiscal policy, monetary policy, or both.

Disposable income is gross income minus taxes plus transfer payment.

Dynamic analysis explains the path from one equilibrium point to another providing a causal process.

Equilibrium refers to a point where market forces cancel each other out, and there is no endogenous force remaining to influence the market.

Externalities are consequences, both positive and negative, which were not brought about by one's choice and action.

Fiat money is a currency without precious metal backing. The value of fiat money stems from the dependability of the government that issues it.

Fiscal policy refers to government intervention in the economy through manipulation of government revenues and disbursements for the purpose of influencing the course of the economy.

GDP (gross domestic product) is the value of final goods and services produced in a country in one year.

Income elasticity is a measure of responsiveness of demand for a good to changes in income. It is equal to the ratio of percentage change in demand to a percentage change in income.

Inferior good has negative income elasticity. The demand for an inferior good declines when income increases.

Inside lag is the time between recognition of the need for a stimulus or restraint and the legislation of the appropriate regulations.

IS schedule is the loci of interest rate-output sets for which the goods market is in equilibrium.

LM schedule is the loci of combinations of interest rates and incomes that result in equilibrium in the money market.

Macroeconomics is the study of aggregated indicators, such as GDP.

Marginal cost is the cost of producing one more unit of a good or service.

Marginal propensity to consume is the change in consumption due to a one-unit change in income.

Marginal revenue is the increase in revenue as a result of selling one more unit of a good or service.

Marginal utility is the utility derived from consumption of one more unit of a good or service.

Monetary policy refers to government intervention in the economy through manipulation of supply of money for the purpose of influencing the course of the economy.

Monetary theory provides theoretical foundations about the behavior of money markets.

Multiplier effect refers to the successive rounds of income-consumption generated by an initial increase in consumption, investment, or government expenditures.

None-exclusion nature of public goods refers to the fact that once the good is provided everybody will benefit from it even if they choose not to pay for it, such as national security.

Outside lag is the time between a policy action and the appearance of its effects in the economy.

Phillips curve refers to the empirical evidence of tradeoff between inflation and unemployment.

Rational expectations is a hypothesis based on the notion that economic agents behave according to the statistical concept of expected value.

Say's Law of Market states that production creates its demand.

Transfer payment is any payment made by the government to the private sector for social or welfare purposes.

Velocity of money represents the average number of times money changes hand in a year.

Notes

Chapter 1

1. Smith (1776 [2011]).
2. Mun (1630).
3. Locke (1691).
4. Mun (1630).
5. Buer (1921).
6. Jevons (1878).
7. Smith (1776 [2011]).
8. Owen (1817); Sismondi (1819 [1991]).
9. Hume (1748 [2005]).
10. Fisher (1907).
11. Patinkin (1954).
12. Mun (1630).
13. Fisher (1911).
14. Fisher (1911).
15. Hume (1748 [2005]).
16. Naghshpour (2013b).
17. Keynes (1930 [1976]).
18. Hume (1748 [2005]).
19. Smith (1776 [2011]).
20. Smith (1776 [2011]).

Chapter 2

1. Hume (1907).
2. Keynes (1936 [2006]).
3. Ricardo (1817).
4. Smith (1776 [2011]).
5. Smith (1776 [2011]).
6. Naghshpour (2013a).
7. Naghshpour (2013a).
8. Smith (1776 [2011]).
9. Marx (1875).
10. Blanc (1839).

11. Keynes (1936 [2006]).
12. Friedman (1960).
13. Friedman and Schwarz (1963).
14. Simons (1936).
15. Lucas (1980).
16. Friedman (1960).
17. Taylor (1993a).
18. Goodfriend (2003).

Chapter 3

1. cf. Naghshpour (2013a).

Chapter 4

1. Fisher (1911).
2. Kuznets (1934).
3. Baumol (1977).
4. Naghshpour (2013b).
5. Baumol (1977).
6. Keynes (1936 [2006]).
7. Friedman (1964).
8. Stock and Watson (1993).
9. Ball (1998).
10. Alvarez and Lippi (2011).
11. Weeks (2013).
12. Fisher (1911).
13. Kuznets (1934).
14. Bruner and Meltzer (1963).

Chapter 5

1. Epstein (2009).
2. Bernanke (2010).
3. Keynes (1913).
4. Keynes (1936 [2006]).
5. Kahn (1931).
6. Friedman and Heller (1969).
7. Friedman and Heller (1969).
8. Friedman and Heller (1969).

9. Friedman and Heller (1969).
10. Fisher (1907).
11. Hicks (1937).
12. Modigliani (1944).
13. Klein (1947).
14. Samuelson (1948).
15. Hansen (1953).
16. Modigliani (1944).
17. Tobin (1955); Tobin (1969).
18. Robinson (1962).
19. Shackle (1967).
20. Patinkin (1956).
21. Patinkin (1956).
22. Leijonhufvud (1968).

Chapter 6

1. Keynes (1936 [2006]).
2. Pigou (1917).
3. Pigou (1917).
4. Pigou (1917).
5. Pigou (1917).
6. Friedman (1956).
7. Naghshpour (2012b).
8. Friedman (1959).
9. Naghshpour (2013b).
10. Friedman (1956); Friedman (1959).

Chapter 7

1. Friedman (1956).
2. Patinkin (1974).
3. Friedman (1959).
4. Friedman and Friedman (1962); Friedman and Friedman (1980).
5. Friedman and Schwartz (1963).
6. Friedman and Schwartz (1963).
7. Friedman and Schwartz (1963).
8. Naghshpour (2012a).
9. Friedman (1960).
10. Phillips (1958).

11. Phillips (1958).
12. Samuelson and Solow (1960).
13. Friedman (1968).
14. Friedman (1968).
15. Phelps (1967).
16. Lucas (1972); Sargent (1986); Sims (2009).
17. Friedman (1983).
18. Friedman (1968).

Chapter 8

1. Menger (1871).
2. Bohm-Bawerk (1959).
3. Mises (1912).
4. Hayek (1935).
5. Naghshpour (2013a).

Chapter 9

1. Muth (1961).
2. Muth (1961).
3. Naghshpour (2012b).
4. Phillips (1958).
5. Sargent and Wallace (1976).
6. Muth (1961).
7. Muth (1961).
8. Friedman (1953).
9. Friedman (1953).

Chapter 10

1. Taylor (1993a).
2. Friedman (1967).
3. McCallum (1998).
4. McCallum (1999).
5. Taylor (1993a).
6. Taylor (2000).
7. Friedman (1967).
8. Taylor (2000).

9. Kydland and Prescott (1977); Barro and Gordon (1983); Blanchard and Fischer (1989).
10. Taylor (1993b).
11. Taylor (1993a).
12. Taylor (1993a).
13. Taylor (1993a).
14. Taylor (1993a).

Chapter 11

1. Friedman and Schwartz (1963).
2. Friedman (1956).
3. Friedman and Schwartz (1963).
4. Friedman (1956).
5. Friedman and Meiselman (1963).
6. Ando and Modigliani (1965).
7. Tobin and Swan (1969).
8. Friedman and Schwartz (1963).
9. Friedman and Schwartz (1963).
10. Friedman and Schwartz (1963).
11. Friedman (1966).
12. Friedman and Meiselman (1963).
13. Friedman and Meiselman (1963).
14. Friedman and Meiselman (1963).
15. Hester (1964).
16. Ando and Modigliani (1965).
17. Wooldridge (2009).
18. Ando and Modigliani (1965).
19. Friedman and Meiselman (1963).
20. DePrano and Mayer (1965).
21. DePrano and Mayer (1965).
22. Friedman and Meiselman (1963).
23. DePrano and Mayer (1965).
24. Friedman and Schwartz (1963).
25. Friedman (1966).
26. Moore (1979).
27. Hamburger (1977).
28. Mises (1966).
29. Summers (2001).
30. Wainhouse (1984).

31. Lucas (1996).
32. McCandless and Weber (1995).
33. Friedman and Schwartz (1963).
34. Sargent (1986).
35. Sargent and Wallace (1976).
36. Acemoglu and Scott (1994).
37. Bryant, Hooper, and Mann (1993).
38. Naghshpour and St. Marie (2008).
39. Naghshpour and St. Marie (2009).

Chapter 12

1. DePrano and Mayer (1965).

References

Acemoglu, D., & Scott, A. (1994). Consumer confidence and rational expectations: Are agents' beliefs consistent with the theory? *The Economic Journal 104*(22), 1–19.

Alvarez, F., & Lippi, F. (2011, November). *Persistent liquidity effects and long run money demand* (NBER Working Paper No. 17566). Cambridge, MA.

Ando, A., & Modigliani, F. (1965). The relative stability of monetary velocity and the investment multiplier. *The American Economic Review 55*(4), 693–728.

Ball, L. (1998). *Another look at long run money demand* (NBER Working Paper No. 6597). Johns Hopkins University Working Paper.

Barro, R. J., & Gordon, D. B. (1983). Rules, discretion and reputation in a model of monetary policy. *Journal of Monetary Economics 12*, 101–122.

Baumol W. J. (1977). *Economic theory and operations analysis* (4th ed.). Englewood Cliffs, NJ: Prentice-Hall.

Bernanke, B. (2010). *Central bank independence, transparency, and accountability.* Speech at the Institute for Monetary and Economic Studies International Conference, Bank of Japan, Tokyo, Japan.

Blanc, L. (1839 [1848]). The organization of labor. In J. A. D. Marriott (Ed.), *The French Revolution of 1848 in its economic aspect*. Oxford.

Blanchard, O., & Fischer, S. (1989). *Lectures in macroeconomics*. Cambridge, MA: MIT Press.

Bohm-Bawerk, E. Von. (1959 [2012]). *Capital and interest: A critical history of economic theory. Create space independent publishing platform.* London: Macmillan.

Bruner, K., & Meltzer, A. H. (1963). The place of financial intermediaries in the transmission of monetary policy. *American Economic Review 53*, 372–382.

Bryant, R., Hooper, P., & Mann, C. (1993). *Evaluating policy regimes: New research in empirical economics*. Washington, DC: The Brookings Institution.

Buer, M. C. (1921). The trade depression following the Napoleonic wars. *Economica 2*, 159–179.

Cantillon, R. (1720 [2001]). *Essay on the nature of commerce in general.* Transaction Publishers.

DePrano, M., & Mayer, T. (1965). Test of the relative importance of autonomous expenditures and money. *American Economic Association 55*(4), 729–752.

Epstein, G. (2009). *Rethinking monetary and fiscal policy: Practical suggestions for monitoring stability while generating employment and poverty reduction* (Working Paper No. 37). International Labour Office.

Fisher, I. (1907). Why has the doctrine of Laissez Faire been abandoned? *Science New Series 25*(627), 18–27.

Fisher, I. (1911). *The purchasing power of money: It's determination and relation to credit, interest, and crises.* New York, NY: The Macmillan Co.

Friedman, M. (1953). *Essays in positive economics.* Chicago, IL: University of Chicago Press.

Friedman, M. (1956). The quantity theory of money, a restatement. In M. Friedman (Ed.), *Studies in the quantity theory of money.* Chicago, IL: University of Chicago Press.

Friedman, M. (1959). The demand for money: Some theoretical and empirical results. *Journal of Political Economy 67,* 327–351.

Friedman, M. (1960). *A program for monetary stability.* New York, NY: Fordham University Press.

Friedman, M. (1964). Reports on selected bureau programs. In NBER Chapters, *The Great Contraction, 1929–1933* (pp. 66–95). National Bureau of Economic Research, Inc.

Friedman, M. (1966). Interest rates and the demand for money. *Journal of Law and Economics 9,* 71–85.

Friedman, M. (1967). The monetary theory and policies of Henry Simons. *Journal of Law and Economics 10,* 1–13.

Friedman, M. (1968). The role of monetary policy. *The American Economic Review (March) 58*(1), 1–17.

Friedman, M. (1983). Monetarism in rhetoric and in practice. *Bank of Japan Monetary and Economic Studies 1,* 1–14.

Friedman, M., & Friedman, R. (1962). *Capitalism and freedom.* Chicago, IL: University of Chicago Press.

Friedman, M., & Friedman, R. (1980). *Free to choose.* New York, NY: Harcourt Brace Jovanovich.

Friedman, M., & Heller, W. W. (1969). *Monetary vs. fiscal policy: A dialogue.* New York, NY: Norton.

Friedman, M., & Meiselman, D. (1963). *The relative stability of monetary velocity and the investment multiplier in the United States, 1897–1958.* Chicago, IL: University of Chicago Press.

Friedman, M., & Schwartz, A. J. (1963). *A monetary history of the United States, 1867–1960.* Princeton, NJ: Princeton University Press.

Goodfriend, M. (2003). *Inflation targeting in the United States?* (National Bureau of Economic Research Working Paper 9981). Cambridge, MA.

Hamburger. M. (1977). Behavior of the money stock: Is there a puzzle? *Journal of Monetary Economics 3,* 265–288.

Hansen, A. H. (1953). *A guide to Keynes.* New York, NY: McGraw-Hill.

Hayek, F. A. (1935 [1967]). *Prices and production.* New York, NY: Augustus M. Kelley.

Hester, D. D. (1964). Keynes and the quantity theory: A comment on the Friedman - Meiselman CMC Paper. *The Review of Economics and Statistics 46*(4), 364–368.

Hicks, J. R. (1937). Mr. Keynes and the "Classics": A suggested interpretation. *Econometrica 5*(2), 147–159.

Hume, D. (1748 [2005]). *Essays, moral, political, and literary.* Retrieved September 11, 2005, from Indianapolis: The Online Library of Liberty: http://files.libertyfund.org/files/704/Hume_0059.pdf#page=4

Hume, D. (1907). *Essays: Moral, political and literary.* New York, NY: Longmans, Green, and Co.

Jevons, W. S. (1878). Commercial crises and sun-spots. *Nature 19,* 33–37.

Kahn, R. F. (1931). The relation of home investment to unemployment. *The Economic Journal 41*(162), 173–198.

Keynes, J. M. (1913 [1982]). *Indian currency and finance.* London and Basingstoke: Macmillan and Cambridge University Press.

Keynes, J. M. (1930 [1976]). *A treatise on money.* Brooklyn, NY: Ams Pr Inc.

Keynes, J. M. (1936 [2006]). *The general theory of employment, interest and money.* Delhi, IN: Atlantic Publishers and Distributors.

Klein, L. R. (1947). *The Keynesian revolution.* London, UK: Macmillan.

Kuznets, S. (1934). *National income, 1929–1932.* National Bureau of economic Research, Inc.

Kydland, F., & Prescott, E. C. (1977). Rules rather than discretion: The inconsistency of optimal plans. *Journal of Political Economy 85,* 473–492.

Leijonhufvud, A. (1968). *On Keynesian economics and the economics of keynes.* London, UK: Oxford University Press.

Locke, J. (1691). *Some considerations of the consequences of the lowering of interest and the raising the value of money.* Retrieved August 1, 2013, from http://socserv2.socsci.mcmaster.ca/~econ/ugcm/3ll3/locke/consid.txt

Lucas, Jr. R. E. (1972). Expectations and the neutrality of money. *Journal of Economic Theory 4*(2), 103–124.

Lucas, Jr. R. E. (1980). Rules, discretion, and the role of the economic advisor. In S. Fischer (Ed.), *Rational Expectations and Economic Policy.* University of Chicago Press.

Lucas, Jr. R. E. (1996). Nobel lecture: Monetary neutrality. *Journal of Political Economy 104*(4), 661–682.

Marx, K. (1875). *Critique of the Gotha programme.* Retrieved August 1, 2013, from http://www.marxists.org/archive/marx/works/1875/gotha/index.htm

McCallum, B. T. (1988). Robustness properties of a rule for monetary policy. *Carnegie-Rochester Conference Series on Public Policy 29*(1), 173–204.

McCallum, B. T. (1999). *Recent developments in monetary policy analysis: The roles of theory and evidence* (National Bureau of Economic Research Working Paper 7088). Cambridge, MA.

McCandless, G. T. Jr., & Weber, E. W. (1995). Some monetary facts. *Federal Reserve Bank Minneapolis Quarterly Review 19*, 2–11.

Menger, C. (1871 [2011]). *Principles of economics*. Terra Libertas Limited.

Mises, L. (1966). *Human action: A treatise on economics*. Chicago, IL: Henry Regnery.

Mises, L. Von. (1912 [2011]). *The theory of money and credit*. Tribeca Books.

Modigliani, F. (1944). Liquidity preference and the theory of interest and money. *Econometrica 12*(1), 45–88.

Moore, B. J. (1979). The endogenous money stock. *Journal of Post Keynesian Economics 2*(1), 49–70.

Mun, T. (1630 [2008]). *England's treasure by foreign trade*. Kessinger Publishing, LLC.

Muth, J. F. (1961). Rational expectations and the theory of price movement. *Econometrica 29*(3), 315–335.

Naghshpour, S. (2012a). Monetary theory and the struggle with discretion versus rule - Based policy. In Majumdar, M. (Ed.), *Fundamental economics, in Encyclopedia of life support systems (EOLSS), developed under the auspices of the UNESCO*. Oxford, UK: Eolss Publishers.

Naghshpour, S. (2012b). *Statistics for economics*. New York, NY: Business Expert Press.

Naghshpour, S. (2013a). *Monetary policy: Government intervention to influence market performance*. New York, NY: Business Expert Press.

Naghshpour, S. (2013b). *The fundamentals of money and financial systems*. New York, NY: Business Expert Press.

Naghshpour, S., & St. Marie, J. J. (2008). Monetary reality and economic adaptability of new entrants to the EU. *International Journal of Monetary Economics and Finance 1*(4), 399–411.

Naghshpour, S., & St. Marie, J. J. (2009). The applicability of the Taylor rule in east Asian countries. *American Journal of Business Research 2*(2), 101–115.

Owen, R. D. (1817[2012]). Report to the committee for the relief of the manufacturing poor. In *The life of Robert Owen*. Ulan Press.

Patinkin, D. (1954). Dichotomies of the pricing process in economic theory. *Economica 21*(82), 113–128.

Patinkin, D. (1956). *Money, interest and prices: An integration of monetary and value theory*. Evanston, IL: Row Peterson.

Patinkin, D, (1974). Friedman on the quantity theory and Keynesian economics. In R. J. Gordon (Ed.), *Milton Friedman's monetary framework: A debate with his critics*. Chicago, IL: University of Chicago Press.

Phelps, E. S. (1967). Phillips curves, expectations of inflation and optimal unemployment over time. *Economica New Series 34*(135), 254–281.

Phillips, A.W. (1958). The Relationship between unemployment and the rate of change of money wages in the United Kingdom 1861–1957. *Economica 25*, 283–299.

Pigou, A. C. (1917). The value of money. *Quarterly Journal of Economics 32*(1), 38–65.

Ricardo, D. (1817 [2004]). *The principles of political economy and taxation*. Dover Publications.

Robinson, J. (1962). *Economic philosophy*. Harmondsworth: Penguin.

Samuelson, P. A. (1948). *Economics*. New York, NY: McGraw - Hill.

Samuelson, P. A., & Solow, R. M. (1960). Analytical aspects of anti - inflation policy. *The American Economic Review 50*(2), 177–194.

Sargent, T. J. (1986). *Rational expectations and inflation*. New York, NY: Harper and Row.

Sargent, T. J., & Wallace, N. (1976). Rational expectations and the theory of economic policy. *Journal of Monetary Economics 2*(2), 169–183.

Shackle, G. L. S. (1967). *The years of high theory*. Cambridge, MA: Cambridge University Press.

Simons, H. C. (1936). Rules versus authorities in monetary policy. *Journal of Political Economy 44*(1), 1–30.

Sims, C. A. (2009). Inflation expectations, uncertainty, the Phillips curve, and monetary policy. In C. J. Fuhrer, J. S. Little, Y. K. Kodrzycki, & G. P. Olivei (Eds.), *Understanding inflation and the implications for monetary policy: A Phillips curve retrospective*. Cambridge, MA: MIT Press.

Sismondi, J. C. L. (1819 [1991]). *New principles of political economy*. C. R. Hyse (Ed.). Piscataway, NJ: Transaction Publishers.

Smith, A. (1776 [2011]). *Wealth of nations*. Books IV–V. London, UK: Methuen & Co., Ltd., Create Space Independent Publishing Platform.

Stock, J. H., & Watson, M. W. (1993). A simple estimator of cointegrating vectors in higher order integrated systems. *Econometrica 61*(4), 783–820.

Summers, L. (2001). The new economy: Background, historical perspective, questions, and speculations. *Economic Review* (4), 11–43.

Taylor, J. B. (1993a). Discretion versus policy rules in practice. *Carnegie-Rochester Conference Series on Public Policy 39*, 195–214.

Taylor, J. B. (1993b). *Macroeconomic policy in a world economy: From econometric design to practical operation*. New York, NY: W.W. Norton.

Taylor, J. B. (2000). Reassessing discretionary fiscal policy. *The Journal of Economic Perspectives 14*(3), 21–36.

Tobin, J. (1955). A dynamic aggregative model. *Journal of Political Economy 63*(2), 103–115.

Tobin, J. (1969). A general equilibrium approach to monetary theory. *Journal of Money, Credit, and Banking (February)* 1(1), 15–29.

Tobin, J., & Swan, C. (1969). Money and permanent income: Some empirical tests. *The American Economic Review 59*(2), 285–295.

Wainhouse, C. E. (1984). Empirical evidence for Hayek's theory of economic fluctuations. In B. N. Siegel (Ed.), *Money in crisis*. San Francisco, CA: Pacific Institute for Public Policy Research.

Weeks, J. (2013). Open economy monetary policy reconsidered. *Review of Political Economy 1*, 57–67.

Wooldridge, J. M. (2009). *Introductory econometrics: A modern approach*. South-Western.

Index

OTHER TITLES FROM THE ECONOMICS COLLECTION

Philip Romero, The University of Oregon and Jeffrey Edwards,
North Carolina A&T State University, Editors

- *Managerial Economics: Concepts and Principles* by Donald Stengel
- *Your Macroeconomic Edge: Investing Strategies for the Post-Recession World* by Philip J. Romero
- *Working with Economic Indicators: Interpretation and Sources* by Donald Stengel
- *Innovative Pricing Strategies to Increase Profits* by Daniel Marburger
- *Regression for Economics* by Shahdad Naghshpour
- *Statistics for Economics* by Shahdad Naghshpour
- *How Strong Is Your Firm's Competitive Advantage?* by Daniel Marburger
- *A Primer on Microeconomics* by Thomas Beveridge
- *Game Theory: Anticipating Reactions for Winning Actions* by Mark L. Burkey
- *A Primer on Macroeconomics* by Thomas Beveridge
- *Economic Decision Making Using Cost Data: A Guide for Managers* by Daniel Marburger
- *The Fundamentals of Money and Financial Systems* by Shahdad Naghshpour
- *International Economics: Understanding the Forces of Globalization for Managers* by Paul Torelli
- *The Economics of Crime* by Zagros Madjd-Sadjadi
- *Money and Banking: An Intermediate Market-Based Approach* by William D. Gerdes

Announcing the Business Expert Press Digital Library

*Concise E-books Business Students Need
for Classroom and Research*

This book can also be purchased in an e-book collection by your library as
- a one-time purchase,
- that is owned forever,
- allows for simultaneous readers,
- has no restrictions on printing, and
- can be downloaded as PDFs from within the library community.

Our digital library collections are a great solution to beat the rising cost of textbooks. e-books can be loaded into their course management systems or onto student's e-book readers.

The **Business Expert Press** digital libraries are very affordable, with no obligation to buy in future years. For more information, please visit **www.businessexpertpress.com/librarians**. To set up a trial in the United States, please contact **Adam Chesler** at *adam.chesler@businessexpertpress.com* for all other regions, contact **Nicole Lee** at *nicole.lee@igroupnet.com*.

www.ingramcontent.com/pod-product-compliance
Lightning Source LLC
Chambersburg PA
CBHW071849200326
41519CB00016B/4295